Big Knits

Big Knits

20 Stylish Designer Knits in Generous Sizes Using Rowan Yarn

Martin Storey

Photographs by Steven Wooster

St. Martin's Griffin
New York

BIG KNITS

Copyright © 2015 by Berry & Bridges Ltd.

www.stmartins.com

Designer Anne Wilson
Editor Katie Hardwicke
Styling Susan Berry
Pattern writing and knitting Penny Hill
Pattern checker Marilyn Wilson
Charts Therese Chynoweth

Library of Congress Cataloging-in-Publication
Data Available Upon Request

ISBN 978-1-250-06191-1

St. Martin's Griffin books may be purchased
for educational, business, or promotional use.
For information on bulk purchases, please
contact Macmillan Corporate and Premium Sales
Department at 1-800-221-7945, extension 5442,
or write specialmarkets@macmillan.com.

First U.S. Edition: May 2015

10 9 8 7 6 5 4 3 2 1

Contents

Introduction

When I was given the brief to design knitwear for larger sizes that would nonetheless look elegant, I was, if I am honest, a bit nervous. Although I have been designing knitwear for longer than perhaps I care to talk about, it was still quite a challenge for me. What sort of shapes should I include? What elements would still look flattering in bigger sizes? What colors work well? What yarns to choose?

I decided to create as much variety as I could—of shape, texture, and style—on the basis that very few women, whatever their size, have a standard body shape, so what suits someone with a large bust and slim hips will not work as well if their figure is the direct opposite of that. I also chose not to depart too far from the kind of designs I naturally gravitate toward—in other words, relatively pared down shapes with an emphasis on interesting texture. I deliberately chose slightly finer yarns, even though they involve more knitting time, because the effect is infinitely more elegant than the much heavier versions.

I am very pleased with the way my designs have translated into the flesh, as it were. The three models for the book all differed in their sizes, shapes, and heights but we found that the knits were equally flattering to all and even the stylist, who is a size 8 (smaller than included in the pattern sizing), found that some of the size 12 garments looked good on her too, worn a little loose.

This all leaves me to think that rather than tell people exactly what size to wear and how to wear it, flexibility is the key!

I am very pleased with how the knits have photographed so beautifully—the models, photography, and styling have done them all justice.

I hope you find some designs in this book that you enjoy wearing and, equally importantly, that you enjoy knitting too!

Finding a style

The designs in this book divide into groups of styles.

WRAPS

The easiest to wear, whatever your body shape or size, is going to be a wrap. I have included four of these in this book, in a variety of yarns. Two of them, the Harmony wrap and the Peace wrap, are knitted in *Kidsilk Haze*, Rowan's ever popular silk and mohair yarn, both of them in delicate lace patterns. They are wide enough and long enough to wrap around in any way you like, and both make light but warm cover-ups for a chilly evening.

Two other wraps, the Relax wrap and the Stroll wrap, are knitted in yarns that show up the lace pattern element more clearly. The Relax wrap is knitted in Rowan's *Fine Art* yarn, which has a subtle self-stripe, while the Stroll wrap is knitted in *Kid Classic*, making it both very warm but also light.

Harmony wrap

Peace wrap

Stroll wrap

Relax wrap

BOLEROS, SHRUGS, AND CAPES

These useful cover-ups are eternally popular but they will probably work best on those with a smaller bust and wider hips, for example.

They take less yarn than most patterns, they look stylish, and they can provide much needed warmth on a cool summer evening, while helping to mask upper arms.

I created some quite different versions on this theme. The Harmony cape is a very simple curved shape that simply slips over the head and can be worn slightly off the shoulder, if preferred. In *Kidsilk Haze* it is exquisitely lacy and very light to wear, and is great for an evening out. In cream, it would also make a lovely cover-up for a winter wedding!

The Hush shrug, knitted in my favorite Rowan *Wool Cotton 4ply*, is much less formal and with long sleeves works just as well in winter or summer. You could wear it with a sleeveless summer dress (like the model's) or over a t-shirt with pants in the summer, or over a loose shirt and skirt in the winter. The shawl collar is flattering, as is the low curved back and wide rib.

The Tranquil shrug, also in *Wool Cotton 4ply*, is similar but with short sleeves.

The Breeze bolero is a very simple little shrug, with slightly longer sleeves, knitted in Rowan *Alpaca Colour*, a lovely, soft self-striped yarn. It is an edge-to-edge design, which could also tie with a pretty silk ribbon, if you wish.

Hush shrug

Harmony cape

Tranquil shrug

Breeze bolero

LONGER LENGTH DESIGNS

These styles suit people who like to wear designs that cover their hips. The Seashore tunic is a simple design to knit, but gains its impact from the self-striped yarn, which is the thicker, Aran version of the Rowan *Fine Art* yarn. A wide scoop neck is flattering, and the patch pockets at the hem help to lengthen the look.

The Shingle cardigan is a great design for most figure shapes, as the gently flaring hem and the low v-neck will flatter everyone. Buttoning at the top with three buttons, the lower part of the cardigan naturally divides, which helps to disguise wide hips, while the lower neckline is flattering to anyone with a larger bust.

The Coast coat is the longest design in the book, coming to mid-thigh. With its all-over cable design in Rowan *Wool Cotton*, it is very stretchy, making it very accommodating for all figure types.

The Stroll tunic is knitted in *Kidsilk Haze*, which makes it both very soft and quite stretchy and, although lacy, surprisingly warm. The simple long length tunic shape is enhanced with a really beautiful heart-motif lace design, which helps to break up the expanse of knitting, and the large, softly rolled low collar is also very flattering. It looks good over pants (casual or smart) or with a straight skirt.

Seashore tunic

Stroll tunic

Shingle cardigan

Coast coat

MID-LENGTH DESIGNS

The Ocean vest is a favorite of mine as it is very flexible. Wear it casually with jeans or a t-shirt or dress it up, layered, over a simple floral print dress. Wearing it with the lower buttons not done up gives it an attractive slight flare, which is ideal for those with a bigger waistline. The cable shows up really well in a yarn like *Wool Cotton* which, while soft, has a naturally crisp finish.

The Pacific slipover is a great casual cover up, with a lovely textured pattern, in Rowan *Pure Wool 4ply*, which shows it up to advantage. Just right for layering over a shirt, worn with pants or a skirt.

The Rest cardigan is another really good textured design, this one with a simple 4-stitch cable, and an optional tie belt. Its shawl collar is softly flattering, and the shorter sleeves make it ideal as a mid-season garment. Rowan *Pure Wool 4ply* shows up the cable particularly well.

Ocean vest

Pacific slipover

Rest cardigan

WIDER, SHORTER SHAPES

I have included two quite boxy cardigan designs and a hip-bone length sweater. These look particularly good on taller women, worn with pants or a long skirt.

The Serene cardigan is very simple but has a lovely embroidered design on the collar, which is both low cut (flattering to those with shorter necks) and draws attention to the face.

The Weekender cardigan is a more casual design, great for wearing with jeans. It has a very generous loose fit and skims the hip bone. Knitted in Rowan's *Fine Art Aran* yarn, it is wonderfully warm for winter.

The Calm sweater, knitted in Rowan *Kid Classic*, is very straightforward, but its contrast border and cuffs give it a great finish, as does the duplicate stitch flower pattern on the front. If embroidery is beyond you, this sweater looks equally great plain.

Serene cardigan

Calm sweater

Weekender cardigan

Getting the right fit

You need to take accurate body measurements before you start. Get a friend to measure you around your bust, around your hips (widest point), the length from your back neck to the top of your hips, and your arm length (from the neck to the wrist). Draw these out on a diagram so you have them to hand.

The patterns in this book are designed using the bust measurement as the basic starting point, so choose a size that fits your bust size from the measurements at the start of each pattern and then check to see if any other measurements for length to shoulder and length of sleeve match your measurements, too.

ALLOWING FOR EASE
Each pattern will allow some "ease." In other words, the design has a bust measurement at the top and then a larger measurement, which is the finished size of the actual garment.If you like to wear your clothes loose, you may need to go up a size on your bust measurement (or if you need to accommodate wider hips).

GETTING THE GAUGE RIGHT
Whatever size you choose, it is vital that your knitted pieces measure the same as the pieces in the relevant pattern. Each pattern gives you the gauge used in the design, and yours needs to match. You can test this very simply by knitting a small square before you start the main design, and then measuring the stitches and rows over 10in/4cm, as described in the pattern. If you get more rows and stitches than specified, your gauge is tighter and you need to try again using a size larger needles; if you get fewer rows and stitches, your gauge is looser and you need to try again using smaller needles.

MINOR PATTERN ALTERATIONS
It is easy to lengthen or shorten the body of a garment when there are no increases in that part of the pattern, so any design with straight boxy sides can be lengthened or shortened by adding or subtracting the appropriate number of rows (use the gauge square information to work out how many rows you need to add or subtract) to achieve the length you want.

Pattern pieces with shaping in them are less easy to alter as you have to redistribute the increases or decreases accordingly. For example, if you want to shorten a sleeve, your increases will need to be made at shorter intervals than specified on the pattern, and vice versa to lengthen the sleeve. As sleeves are knitted from the cuff to the shoulder, you need to make sure you have made the same number of increases on your knitting as are specified on the pattern at the point where you start to create the armhole. Less complicated length changes for a sleeve would be to make a shorter cuff or to add a longer one. If in doubt as to how to redistribute increases or decreases, consult an experienced knitter.

The
projects

Breeze bolero

Harmony
cape

Harmony
wrap

Seashore tunic

Ocean vest

Stroll tunic

Stroll
wrap

Hush shrug

Weekender jacket

Clear hat

Clear fingerless gloves

Shingle cardigan

Pacific slipover

Rest cardigan

Tranquil shrug

Calm
sweater

Relax
wrap

Coast coat

51

Peace wrap

Serene cardigan

The patterns

Breeze bolero

This very simple stockinette stitch bolero is knitted in the self-striped Rowan *Alpaca Colour* yarn. It comes to just below the bust, and is designed to be worn edge to edge, but you could add matching fine silk or velvet ribbons to give it a tie-front if you prefer.

FINISHED SIZE
To fit bust

36	38	40	42	44	46	in
92	97	102	107	112	117	cm

ACTUAL MEASUREMENTS
Bust

40	42	44	46½	49	50¾	in
102	107	112	118	124	129	cm

Length center at back

13	13¾	14	14½	15½	15¾	in
33	35	36	37	39	40	cm

YARN
5(6:6:7:7:8:8) x 1¾oz/131yd balls of Rowan *Alpaca Colour* in Jasper 134

NEEDLES
Circular size 6 (4mm) needle
Pair of size 6 (4mm) knitting needles

GAUGE
22 sts and 30 rows to 4in/10cm square over St st using size 6 (4mm) needles, or size to obtain correct gauge.

ABBREVIATIONS
See page 133.

BACK
Using size 6 (4mm) circular needle, cast on 34(40:46:52:58:64) sts.
P 1 row.
Beg with a k row, cont in St st.
Cast on 8 sts at beg of next 10 rows.
114(120:126:132:138:144) sts.
Beg with a k row, work 32(34:36:38:40:42) rows in St st.

SHAPE CAP SLEEVES
1st row Cast on 15 sts at beg of next 2 rows.
144(150:156:162:168:174) sts.
Work 2 rows.
Next row K25, M1, k to last 25 sts, M1, k25.
Next row P to end.
Next row K26, M1, k to last 26 sts, M1, k26.
Next row P to end.
Next row K27, M1, k to last 27 sts, M1, k27.
Next row P to end.

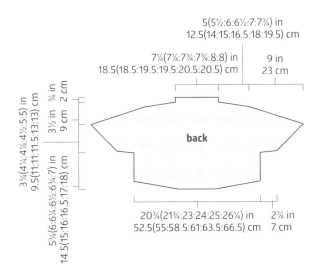

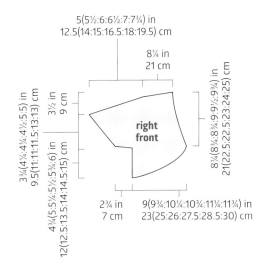

Cont to inc in this way on next row and 21(21:22:22:23:23) foll RS rows, working one more st before first inc and after 2nd inc as before, so ending with a RS row. *194(200:208:214:222:228) sts.* Work 1(3:3:5:5:7) row(s).

SHAPE UPPER ARM
Bind off 5 sts at beg of next 20 rows. *94(100:108:114:122:128) sts.*

SHAPE SHOULDERS
Bind off 9(10:11:12:13:14) sts at beg of next 6 rows. *40(40:42:42:44:44) sts.*
Next row K to end, inc one st at center. *41(41:43:43:45:45) sts.*
Seed st row K1, [p1, k1] to end.
Rep this row 4 times more.
Bind off in seed st.

LEFT FRONT
Using size 6 (4mm) needles, cast on 50(53:56:59:62:65) sts.
P 1 row.
Beg with a k row, work in St st.
Next 2 rows K2, turn, p to end.
Next 2 rows K5, turn, p to end.
Next 2 rows K8, turn, p to end.
Next 2 rows K11, turn, p to end.
Cont in this way, working 3 more sts on every RS row until the foll 2 rows have been worked.
Next 2 rows K50(53:56:59:62:65), turn, p to end.

SHAPE CAP SLEEVE
1st row Cast on 15 sts, k to end. *65(68:71:74:77:80) sts.*
Work 1 row.

SHAPE FRONT NECK
1st row K to last 8 sts, k2tog, k6.
Work 1 row.
Next row K25, M1, k to last 8 sts, k2tog, k6.
Next row P to end.
Next row K26, M1, k to last 8 sts, k2tog, k6.
Next row P to end.
Next row K27, M1, k to last 8 sts, k2tog, k6.
Next row P to end.
Cont to inc in this way on next row and 21(21:22:22:23:23) foll RS rows, working one more st before inc, at the same time work 9(9:10:10:11:11) more decs at neck edge as set, on every foll 4th row then keep neck edge straight, so ending with a RS row. *77(80:83:86:89:92) sts.*
Work 1(3:3:5:5:7) row(s).

SHAPE UPPER ARM
Bind off 5 sts at beg of next and 9 foll RS rows. *27(30:33:36:39:42) sts.*

SHAPE SHOULDER
Bind off 9(10:11:12:13:14) sts at beg of next and foll RS row.
Work 1 row.
Bind off rem 9(10:11:12:13:14) sts.

RIGHT FRONT

Using size 6 (4mm) needles, cast on
50(53:56:59:62:65) sts.
K 1 row.
Beg with a p row, work in St st.
Next 2 rows P2, turn, k to end.
Next 2 rows P5, turn, k to end.
Next 2 rows P8, turn, k to end.
Next 2 rows P11, turn, k to end.
Cont in this way, working 3 more sts on every
WS row until the foll 2 rows have been worked.
Next 2 rows P50(53:56:59:62:65), turn, k to
end.

SHAPE CAP SLEEVE

1st row Cast on 15 sts, p to end.
65(68:71:74:77:80) sts.

SHAPE FRONT NECK

1st row K6, skpo, k to end.
Work 1 row.
Next row K6, skpo, k to last 25 sts, M1, k25.
Next row P to end.
Next row K6, skpo, k to last 26 sts, M1, k26.
Next row P to end.
Next row K6, skpo, k to last 27 sts, M1, k27.
Next row P to end.
Cont to inc in this way on next row and
21(21:22:22:23:23) foll RS rows, working one
more st after inc at the same time work work
9(9:10:10:11:11) more decs at neck edge as
set, on every foll 4th row then keep neck
edge straight, so ending with a RS row.
77(80:83:86:89:92:95:98) sts.
Work 2(4:4:6:6:8) rows.

SHAPE UPPER ARM

Bind off 5 sts at beg of next and 9 foll WS
rows. *27(30:33:36:39:42) sts.*

SHAPE SHOULDER

Bind off 9(10:11:12:13:14) sts at beg of next
and foll WS row.
Work 1 row.
Bind off rem 9(10:11:12:13:14) sts.

LOWER BACK EDGING

With RS facing, using size 6 (4mm) circular
needle, pick up and k115(121:127:133:139:145)
sts evenly along lower edge.
Seed st row K1, [p1, k1] to end.

Rep this row 4 times more.
Bind off in seed st.

LEFT FRONT EDGING

With RS facing and size 6 (4mm) circular
needle, starting at neck edge pick up and
50(53:56:59:62:65) sts to end of front
shaping, then k45(46:47:48:49:50) sts to side
edge. *95(99:103:107:111:115) sts.*
Seed st row K1, [p1, k1] to end.
Rep this row 4 times more.
Bind off in seed st.

RIGHT FRONT EDGING

With RS facing and size 6 (4mm) circular
needle, starting at side edge, pick up and
k45(46:47:48:49:50) to end of front shaping,
then k50(53:56:59:62:65) sts to shoulder.
95(99:103:107:111:115) sts.
Seed st row K1, [p1, k1] to end.
Rep this row 4 times more.
Bind off in seed st.

SLEEVE EDGING

Join shoulder, upper arm, and edging seams.
With RS facing, using size 6 (4mm) needles,
pick up and k73(77:81:87:91:95:99) sts evenly
around armhole edge.
Seed st row K1, [p1, k1] to end.
Rep this row 4 times more.
Bind off in seed st.

FINISHING

Join side and sleeve edging seams.

Harmony cape

If you love lacy designs then this elegant little cape in Rowan *Kidsilk Haze* is just the thing. It has a simple, deep ribbed neck, loose enough for it to be worn slightly off the shoulder (as modeled) and the cape flares out gently from this. The lace and cable pattern is a relatively simple 24-st repeat.

FINISHED SIZE
ONE SIZE
Length
18in/46cm

YARN
Five x 1oz/229yd balls of Rowan *Kidsilk Haze* in Majestic 589

NEEDLES
Pair each of size 2 (2.75mm) and size 2–3 (3mm) knitting needles
Long size 3 (3.25mm) circular needle
Cable needle

GAUGE
24½ sts and 32 rows to 4in/10cm square over patt using size 3 (3.25mm) needles, or size to obtain correct gauge.

ABBREVIATIONS
C4F = slip next 2 sts onto cable needle and hold at front of work, k2, then k2 from cable needle.
See also page 133.

BACK AND FRONT ALIKE
Using size 3 (3.25mm) circular needle, cast on 280 sts.
Work backward and forward in rows.
Row 1 K20, * [work across 24-st patt rep] twice, then work first 6 sts of patt rep, k39; rep from * once, [work across 24-st patt rep] twice, then work first 6 sts of patt rep, k20.

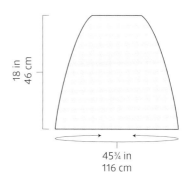

18 in
46 cm

45¾ in
116 cm

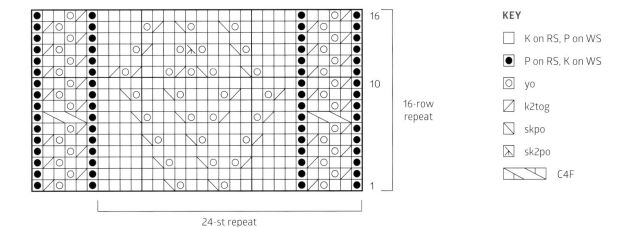

KEY

☐ K on RS, P on WS

● P on RS, K on WS

⊡ yo

⟋ k2tog

⟍ skpo

⅄ sk2po

⟋⟍ C4F

16-row repeat

24-st repeat

Row 2 P20, * [work across 24-st patt rep] twice, then work last 6 sts of patt rep, p39; rep from * once, [work across 24-st patt rep] twice, then work last 6 sts of patt rep, p20.
These 2 rows set the patt panels with St st between.
Work a further 12 rows.
Dec row K18, k2tog, * patt 54, skpo, k35, k2tog; rep from * once more, patt 54, skpo, k18.
Work 5 rows with sts as set.
Dec row 2 K17, k2tog, * patt 54, skpo, k33, k2tog; rep from * once more, patt 54, skpo, k17.
Work 5 rows with sts as set.
Dec row 3 K16, k2tog, * patt 54, skpo, k31, k2tog; rep from * once more, patt 54, skpo, k17.
Work 5 rows with sts as set.
Cont in this way, decreasing 6 sts on the next and 14 foll 6th rows. *172 sts.*
Work 5 rows with sts as set.
Dec row 19 K2tog, * patt 54, sk2po; rep from * once more, patt 54, skpo. *166 sts.*
Work 5 rows with sts as set.
Change to size 2–3 (3mm) needles.
Dec row 20 [K1, p1] 5 times, * k2tog, [p1, k1] 4 times, p1; rep from * 12 times, k2tog, [p1, k1] 5 times, p1. *152 sts.*
Rib row 1 [K1, p1] to end.
Rep this row for 2in/5cm.
Change to size 2 (2.75mm) needles.
Work a further 1¾in/4cm.
Using size 2–3 (3mm) needles, bind off in rib.

FINISHING
Join side seams.

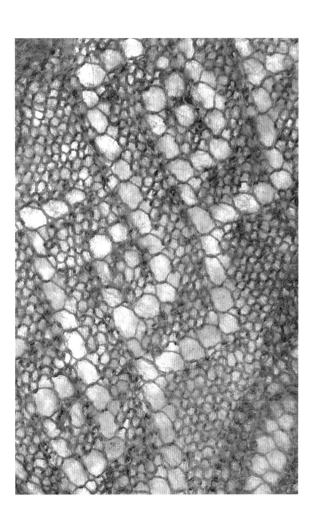

Harmony wrap

Also in Rowan *Kidsilk Haze*, this is an even simpler take on the stitch design used in the Harmony cape, as it requires no shaping. Wide and long, it provides the perfect summer evening cover-up, but will also work beautifully over a more formal dress.

FINISHED SIZE
ONE SIZE
17¼in/44cm by 66in/170cm long

YARN
Four x 1oz/229yd balls of Rowan *Kidsilk Haze* in Splendour 579

NEEDLES
Pair of size 3 (3.25mm) knitting needles
Cable needle

GAUGE
24½ sts and 32 rows to 4in/10cm square over patt using size 3 (3.25mm) needles, or size to obtain correct gauge.

ABBREVIATIONS
C4F = slip next 2 sts onto cable needle and hold at front of work, k2, then k2 from cable needle.
See also page 133.

FIRST SIDE
Using size 3 (3.25mm) needles, cast on 108 sts.
Row 1 K1, p1, k1, [work across 24-st patt rep] 4 times, then work first 6 sts of patt rep, k1, p1, k1.
Row 2 K1, p1, k1, work last 6 sts of patt rep, then [work across 24-st patt rep] 4 times, k1, p1, k1.
These 2 rows set the patt panels with seed st at each end.
Work even until piece measures 33½in/85cm from cast-on edge, ending with a 14th row.
Leave these sts on a spare needle.

SECOND SIDE
Work to match first side, ending with a 15th row.
With RS together and needles pointing in the same direction, using a larger needle, bind one st off from each needle together.

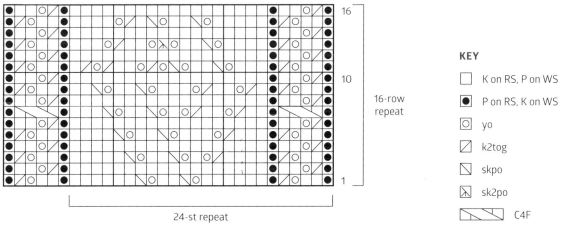

16-row
repeat

24-st repeat

KEY

☐ K on RS, P on WS

⬤ P on RS, K on WS

⊡ yo

⬩ k2tog

⬩ skpo

⬩ sk2po

▧ C4F

Seashore tunic

Knitted in stockinette stitch in Rowan *Fine Art Aran* (the similarly self-striped, cozier cousin to *Fine Art*), the Seashore tunic is perfect for fall or winter walks. It has a very relaxed tunic shape to the top of the thigh, and two large patch pockets with a garter stitch trim.

FINISHED SIZE

To fit bust

36–40	42–44	46–48	in
92–102	107–112	117–122	cm

ACTUAL MEASUREMENTS

Bust

43	48	52¾	in
109	122	134	cm

Length to shoulder

31½	32¼	33	in
80	82	84	cm

Sleeve length

15in/38cm

YARN

9(10:11) x 3½oz/186yd balls of Rowan *Fine Art Aran* in Bachata 551

NEEDLES

Pair each of size 6 (4mm) and size 7 (4.5mm) knitting needles

GAUGE

19 sts and 25 rows to 4in/10cm square over St st using size 7 (4.5mm) needles, or size to obtain correct gauge.

NOTE

When working with *Fine Art Aran*, use 2 balls at a time and work 2 rows from each ball.

ABBREVIATIONS

See page 133.

BACK

Using size 6 (4mm) needles, cast on 106(118:130) sts.
K 5 rows.
Change to size 7 (4.5mm) needles.
Beg with a k row, cont in St st until back measures 30¾(31½:32¼)in/78(80:82)cm from cast-on edge, ending with a p row.

SHAPE UPPER ARMS
Bind off 4(5:6) sts at beg of next 4 rows.

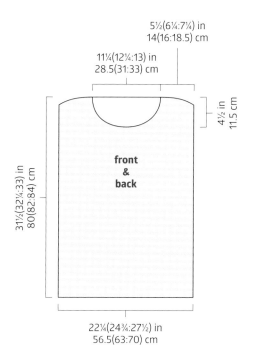

5½(6¼:7¼) in
14(16:18.5) cm

11¼(12¼:13) in
28.5(31:33) cm

4½ in
11.5 cm

**front
&
back**

31½(32¼:33) in
80(82:84) cm

22¼(24¾:27½) in
56.5(63:70) cm

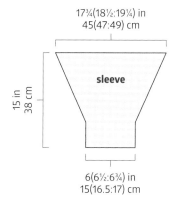

17¾(18½:19¼) in
45(47:49) cm

15 in
38 cm

sleeve

6(6½:6¾) in
15(16.5:17) cm

SHAPE SHOULDERS
Bind off 9(10:11) sts at beg of next 4 rows.
Leave rem 54(58:62) sts on a holder.

FRONT
Work as given for Back until 20 rows fewer
have been worked than on back to upper arm
shaping.

SHAPE FRONT NECK
Next row K46(50:54), turn and work on these
sts for first side of neck.
Next row Bind off 2 sts, p to end.
Next row K to end.
Rep the last 2 rows 8 times more.
Next row Bind off 2 sts, p to end.
26(30:34) sts.

SHAPE UPPER ARM
Bind off 4(5:6) sts at beg of next and foll RS
row.

SHAPE SHOULDER
Bind off 9(10:11) sts at beg of next row.
Work 1 row.
Bind off rem 9(10:11) sts.
With RS facing, place center 14(18:22) sts on
a holder, rejoin yarn to rem sts, k to end.
Next row P to end.
Next row Bind off 2 sts, k to end.
Rep the last 2 rows 9 times more.
26(30:34) sts.

SHAPE UPPER ARMS
Bind off 4(5:6) sts at beg of next and foll
WS row.

SHAPE SHOULDER
Bind off 9(10:11) sts at beg of next row.
Work 1 row.
Bind off rem 9(10:11) sts.

SLEEVES
Using size 6 (4mm) needles, cast on 47(50:53)
sts.
Row 1 (RS) K2, [p1, k2] to end.
Row 2 P2, [k1, p2] to end.
These 2 rows form the rib.
Work a further 21 rows.
Inc row P2, [k1, M1, p2] to end.
62(66:70) sts.

Work a further 24 rows with rib as reset.
Change to size 7 (4.5mm) needles.
Beg with a k row, cont in St st.
Work 4 rows.
Inc row K4, M1, k to last 4 sts, M1, k4.
Work 3 rows.
Rep the last 4 rows 10 times more.
84(88:92) sts.
Bind off.

POCKETS (make 2)
Using size 6 (4mm) needles, cast on 35 sts.
K 3 rows.
Change to size 7 (4.5mm) needles.
Row 1 K to end.
Row 2 K2, p31, k2.
Rep the last 2 rows 21 times and the first row
again.
Change to size 6 (4mm) needles.
K 4 rows.
Bind off.

NECKBAND
Join right upper arm and shoulder seam.
Using size 6 (4mm) needles, pick up and
k32(34:36) sts down left front neck, k across
14(18:22) sts from front neck holder, pick
up and k32(34:36) sts up RS of front neck,
54(58:62) sts from back neck.
132(144:156) sts.
K 4 rows.
Bind off.

FINISHING
Join left upper arm and shoulder seams. Sew on
sleeves. Join side and sleeve seams.
Sew on pockets.

Ocean vest

This design has great classic simplicity. The sleeveless, slightly elongated shape allows you to wear it over pants and a pretty top for a casual yet smart look, but it would dress up effortlessly worn over a printed flowery dress for a summer party. Leaving the bottom few buttons open gives you more flexibility if your waistline is on the generous side, as does the peplum style base to the vest.

The cable pattern shows up beautifully in the yarn (Rowan *Wool Cotton 4ply*), which is soft to wear but still crisp enough to give real clarity to the stitches.

FINISHED SIZE

To fit bust

36-38	40-42	44-46	in
92-97	102-107	112-117	cm

ACTUAL MEASUREMENTS

Bust

40	44¼	48¼	in
102	112	122	cm

Length to shoulder

24½	25¼	26	in
62	64	66	cm

YARN

8(9:10:11) x 1¾oz/197yd balls of Rowan *Wool Cotton 4ply* in Antique 480

NEEDLES

Pair each of size 2–3 (3mm) and size 3 (3.25mm) knitting needles
Circular size 2–3 (3mm) and size 3 (3.25mm) needles
Cable needle

EXTRAS

Six buttons

GAUGE

28 sts and 36 rows to 4in/10cm square over St st using size 3 (3.25mm) needles, or size to obtain correct gauge.
Panel A measures 1½in/3.5cm
Panel B measures 3½in/8.5cm

ABBREVIATIONS

T2R = slip next st onto cable needle and hold at back of work, k1tbl, then p1 from cable needle.
T2L = slip next st onto cable needle and hold at front of work, p1, then k1tbl from cable needle.
Cr4R = slip next 2 sts onto cable needle and hold at back of work, k2, then p2 from cable needle.
Cr4L = slip next 2 sts onto cable needle and hold at front of work, p2, then k2 from cable needle.
C4B = slip next 2 sts onto cable needle and

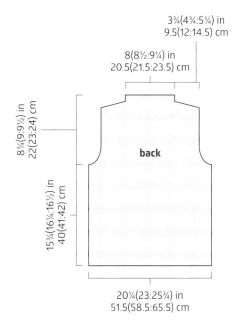

3¾(4¾:5¾) in
9.5(12:14.5) cm

8(8½:9¼) in
20.5(21.5:23.5) cm

8¾(9:9½) in
22(23:24) cm

back

15¾(16¼:16½) in
40(41:42) cm

20¼(23:25¾) in
51.5(58.5:65.5) cm

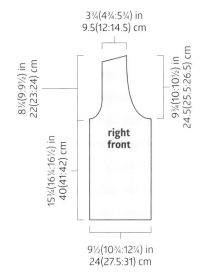

3¾(4¾:5¾) in
9.5(12:14.5) cm

8¾(9:9½) in
22(23:24) cm

9¾(10:10½) in
24.5(25.5:26.5) cm

**right
front**

15¾(16¼:16½) in
40(41:42) cm

9½(10¾:12¼) in
24(27.5:31) cm

hold at back of work, k2, then k2 from cable
needle.
C4F = slip next 2 sts onto cable needle and
hold at front of work, k2, then k2 from cable
needle.
C5R = slip next 2 sts onto cable needle and
hold at back of work, k3, then p2 from cable
needle.
C5L = slip next 3 sts onto cable needle and
hold at front of work, p2, then k3 from cable
needle.
C6B = slip next 3 sts onto cable needle and
hold at back of work, k3, then k3 from cable
needle.
See also page 133.

BACK

Using size 3 (3.25mm) circular needle, cast on
171(197:223) sts.
1st row K3, [p2, T2R, k1, T2L, p2, k4] to end,
ending last rep k3.
2nd row P3, [k2, p1, [k1, p1] twice, k2, p4]
to end, ending last rep p3.
3rd row K3, [p1, T2R, p1, k1, p1, T2L, p1, k4]
to end, ending last rep k3.
4th row P3, [k1, p1, [k2, p1] twice, k1, p4]
to end, ending last rep p3.
5th row K3, [T2R, p2, k1, p2, T2L, k4] to end,
ending last rep k3.
6th row P3, [k4, p1, k4, p4] to end, ending
last rep p3.
These 6 rows form the welt patt.
Work a further 48 rows, inc 19(17:15) sts
across last row. *190(214:238) sts.*
Work in patt from Chart.
Row 1 [P2, work across row 1 patt panel A]
1(2:3) time(s), [work across row 1 patt panel
B, work across row 1 patt panel A] 3 times,
work across row 1 patt panel B, [work across
row 1 patt panel A, p2] 1(2:3) time(s).
Row 2 [K2, work across row 2 patt panel A]
1(2:3) time(s), [work across row 2 patt panel
B, work across row 2 patt panel A] 3 times,
work across row 2 patt panel B, [work across
row 2 patt panel A, k2] 1(2:3) time(s).
These 2 rows set the position for the Charts.
Cont in patt until back measures 15¾(16¼:16½)
in/40(41:42)cm from cast-on edge, ending with
a WS row.

Patt Panel A

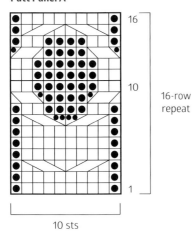

16

10

16-row
repeat

1

10 sts

KEY

☐ K on RS, P on WS

● P on RS, K on WS

Cr4R

Cr4L

C4F

C4B

C5R

C5L

C6B

Patt Panel B

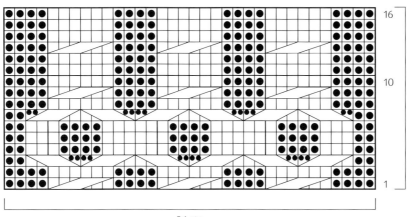

16

10

16-row
repeat

1

34 sts

SHAPE ARMHOLES

Bind off 12 sts at beg of next 2 rows.
Dec one st at each end of the next and 9 foll
RS rows. *146(170:194) sts.*
Work even until back measures 24½(25¼:26)
in/62(64:66)cm from cast-on edge, ending with
a WS row.

SHAPE SHOULDERS

Bind off 12(15:18) sts at beg of next 6 rows.
74(80:86) sts.
Change to size 2–3 (3mm) needles.
Next row Patt to end, dec one st at center.
73(79:85) sts.
Next row K1, [p1, k1] to end.
Next row P1, [k1, p1] to end.
Rep the last 2 rows 4 times more.
Bind off in rib.

LEFT FRONT

Using size 3 (3.25mm) needles, cast on
80(93:106) sts.
1st row K3, [p2, T2R, k1, T2L, p2, k4] to end,
ending last rep k3.
2nd row P3, [k2, p1, [k1, p1] twice, k2, p4]
to end, ending last rep p3.
3rd row K3, [p1, T2R, p1, k1, p1, T2L, p1, k4]
to end, ending last rep k3.
4th row P3, [k1, p1, [k2, p1] twice, k1, p4]
to end, ending last rep p3.
5th row K3, [T2R, p2, k1, p2, T2L, k4] to end,
ending last rep k3.
6th row P3, [k4, p1, k4, p4] to end, ending
last rep p3.
These 6 rows form the welt patt.
Work a further 48 rows, inc 10(9:8) sts across

last row. *90(102:114) sts.*
Work in patt from Charts.
Row 1 Work across row 1 patt panel B, work across row 1 patt panel A, work across row 1 patt panel B, [work across row 1 patt panel A, p2] 1(2:3) time(s).
Row 2 [K2, work across row 2 patt panel A] 1(2:3) time(s), work across row 2 patt panel B, work across row 2 patt panel A, work across row 2 patt panel B.
These 2 rows set the position for the Charts.
Cont in patt until front measures 15¾(16¼:16½) in/40(41:42)cm from cast-on edge, ending with a WS row.

SHAPE ARMHOLE AND FRONT NECK
Bind off 12 sts at beg of next 2 rows.
Dec one st at each end of the next and 9 foll RS rows. *46(58:70) sts.*
Keeping armhole edge straight cont to dec at neck edge on every RS row until 36(45:54) sts rem.
Work even until front measures the same as back to shoulder shaping, ending at armhole edge.

SHAPE SHOULDER
Bind off 12(15:18) sts at beg of next and foll RS row.
Work 1 row.
Bind off rem 12(15:18) sts.

RIGHT FRONT
Using size 3 (3.25mm) needles, cast on 80(93:106) sts.
1st row K3, [p2, T2R, k1, T2L, p2, k4] to end, ending last rep k3.
2nd row P3, [k2, p1, [k1, p1] twice, k2, p4] to end, ending last rep p3.
3rd row K3, [p1, T2R, p1, k1, p1, T2L, p1, k4] to end, ending last rep k3.
4th row P3, [k1, p1, [k2, p1] twice, k1, p4] to end, ending last rep p3.
5th row K3, [T2R, p2, k1, p2, T2L, k4] to end, ending last rep k3.
6th row P3, [k4, p1, k4, p4] to end, ending last rep p3.
These 6 rows form the welt patt.
Work a further 48 rows, inc 10(9:8) sts across last row. *90(102:114) sts.*
Work in patt from Charts.

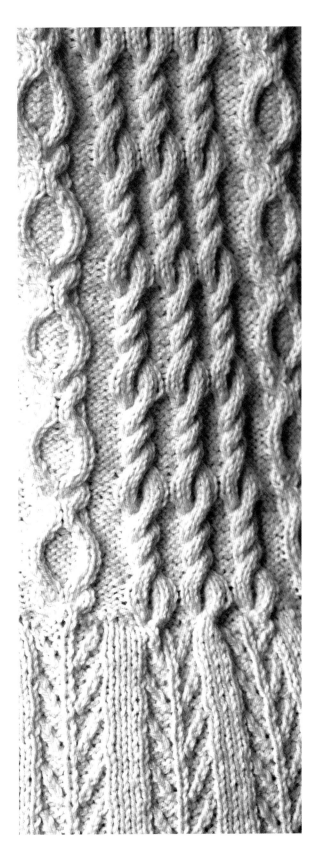

Row 1 [P2, work across row 1 patt panel A] 1(2:3) time(s), work across row 1 patt panel B, work across row 1 patt panel A, work across row 1 patt panel B.
Row 2 Work across row 2 patt panel B, work across row 2 patt panel A, work across row 2 patt panel B, [work across row 2 patt panel A, k2] 1(2:3) time(s).
These 2 rows set the position for the Charts.
Cont in patt until front measures 15¾(16¼:16½) in/40(41:42)cm from cast-on edge, ending with a WS row.

SHAPE ARMHOLE AND FRONT NECK
Bind off 12 sts at beg of next 2 rows.
Dec one st at each end of the next and 9 foll RS rows. *46(58:70) sts.*
Keeping armhole edge straight, cont to dec at neck edge on every RS row until 36(45:54) sts rem.
Work even until front measures the same as back to shoulder shaping, ending at armhole edge.

SHAPE SHOULDER
Bind off 12(15:18) sts at beg of next and foll WS row.
Work 1 row.
Bind off rem 12(15:18) sts.

RIGHT FRONT NECKBAND
With RS facing, using circular size 2–3 (3mm) needle, pick up and k12 sts from right front, pick up and k72(76:80) sts evenly up right front to shoulder.
Next row [P1, k1] to end.
Rep the last row 9 times more.
Bind off in rib.

LEFT FRONT NECKBAND
With RS facing, using circular size 2–3 (3mm) needle, pick up and k72(76:80) sts down left side of front neck, and 12 sts from left front.
Next row [K1, p1] to end.
Rep the last row 9 times more.
Bind off in rib.

BUTTON BAND
With RS facing, using circular size 2–3 (3mm) needle, pick up and k80(86:90) sts down left front to top of welt, then 45 sts to cast-on edge.
Next row K1, [p1, k1] to end.
Next row P1, [k1, p1] to end.
Rep the last 2 rows 4 times more.
Bind off in rib.

BUTTONHOLE BAND
With RS facing, using circular size 2–3 (3mm) needle, pick up and k45 sts up right front to top of welt, then 80(86:90) sts to bound-off edge.
Next row K1, [p1, k1] to end.
Next row P1, [k1, p1] to end.
Rep the last 2 rows once more.
Buttonhole row Rib 4, work 2 tog, yo, [rib 13(14:15), work 2 tog, yo] 5 times, rib to end.
Work a further 5 rows.
Bind off in rib.

ARMBANDS
Join shoulder and neckband seams.
With RS facing, using size 2–3 (3mm) circular needle, pick up and k168(176:184) sts around armhole edge.
Next row [K1, p1] to end.
Rep the last row 9 times more.
Bind off in rib.

FINISHING
Join side seams and armband seams. Sew on buttons.

Stroll tunic

This tunic is both elegant and very relaxed. Knitted in Rowan *Kid Classic* (a very warm, soft yarn) it can be worn casually over pants or dressed up with a straight skirt. The textured pattern of hearts and diamonds helps to break up the expanse of the knitting, and the low softly rolled collar is very flattering.

FINISHED SIZE

To fit bust

36-38	40-42	44-46	in
92-97	102-107	112-117	cm

FINISHED MEASUREMENTS

Bust

40½	45	59¼	in
103	114	125	cm

Length to shoulder

28	29	29½	in
70	72	74	cm

Sleeve length

17¼in/44cm

YARN

10(11:12) x 1¾oz/153yd balls of Rowan *Kid Classic* in Canard 871

NEEDLES

Pair each of size 7 (4.5mm) and size 8 (5mm) knitting needles
Size 7 (4.5mm) and size 8 (5mm) circular needles
Stitch holder

GAUGE

18 sts and 25 rows to 4in/10cm square over patt using size 8 (5mm) needles, or size to obtain correct gauge.

ABBREVIATIONS

Dec 5 = k2tog tbl, k3tog, then pass k2tog tbl stitch over.
Cluster 3 = ytb, slip next 3 sts onto right-hand needle, ytb, slip same 3 sts back onto left-hand needle, ytf, then k3.
See also page 133.

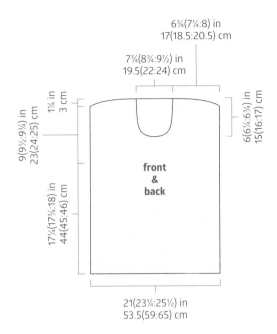

6¾(7¼:8) in
17(18.5:20.5) cm

7¾(8¾:9½) in
19.5(22:24) cm

1¼ in
3 cm

9(9½:9¾) in
23(24:25) cm

6(6¼:6¾) in
15(16:17) cm

front
&
back

17¼(17¾:18) in
44(45:46) cm

21(23¼:25½) in
53.5(59:65) cm

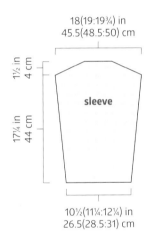

18(19:19¾) in
45.5(48.5:50) cm

1½ in
4 cm

sleeve

17¼ in
44 cm

10½(11¼:12¼) in
26.5(28.5:31) cm

BACK
Using size 7 (4.5mm) needles, cast on
95(105:115) sts.
K 6 rows.
Change to size 8 (5mm) needles.
Cont in border patt.
Row 1 K5(10:15), [yo, skpo, k4, yo, skpo,
k3, k2tog, yo, k5] 5 times, k0(5:10).
Row 2 P to end.
Row 3 K3(8:13), [k2tog, yo, k1tbl, yo, skpo,
k1] 15 times, k2(7:12).
Row 4 P to end.
Work in patt from Chart A.
Row 1 K1(6:11), work across 18 sts before patt
rep of row 1, [work across 18-st patt rep of
row 1] 3 times, work 21 sts after patt rep
then k1(6:11).
Row 2 P1(6:11), work 21 sts before patt rep,
[work across 18-st patt rep] 3 times, work
across 18 sts after patt rep, then p1(6:11).
These 2 rows set the patt.
Work to end of row 20 **.
Work from ** to ** once more.
Beg with a k row work 2 rows in St st.
Work in patt from Chart B.
Row 1 K4(9:14), [work across 28-st patt rep]
3 times, then k7(12:17).
Row 2 P7(12:17), [work across 28-st patt rep]
3 times, then p4(9:14).
These 2 rows set the patt.
Work to end of row 33.
Next row P to end.
Work in patt from Chart C.
Row 1 K6(11:16), [work across 36-st patt rep]
twice, work first 11 sts of patt rep, then
k6(11:16).
Row 2 P6(11:16), work last 11 sts of patt
rep, [work across 36-st patt rep] once, then
p6(11:16).
These 2 rows set the patt.
Work to end of row 15.
Work in patt from Chart D.
Row 1 P10, [work across 10-st patt rep]
8(9:10) times, p5.
Row 2 K5, [work across 10-st patt rep] 8(9:10)
times, k10.
These 2 rows set the patt.
Work to end of row 20.
These 20 rows form the main patt and are
repeated.
Work even until back measures 26½(27¼:28)in/

Chart A

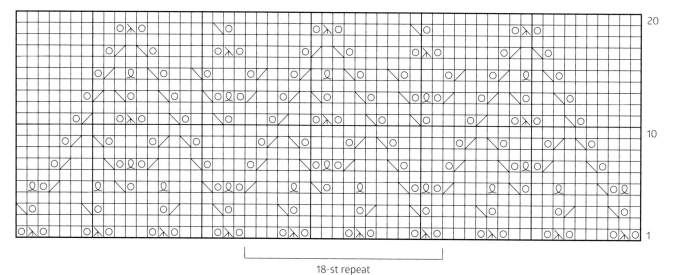

18-st repeat

KEY

☐	K on RS, P on WS
ℚ	k1 tbl
⊙	yo
Ⓜ	M1
⁄	k2tog
＼	skpo
⅄	sk2po
⑤	dec 5
⌣	cluster 3
▦	no stitch

Chart B

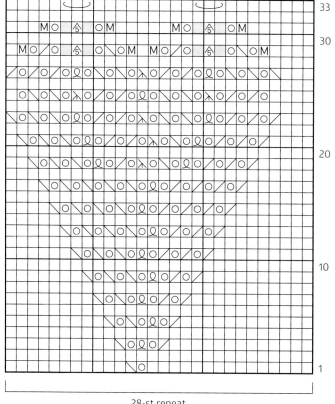

28-st repeat

Chart C

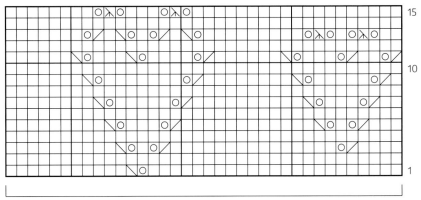

36-st repeat

Chart D

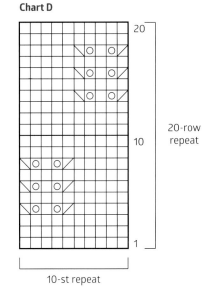

20-row repeat

10-st repeat

67(69:71)cm from cast-on edge, ending with a WS row.

SHAPE UPPER ARMS
Bind off 3 sts at beg of next 8 rows.

SHAPE SHOULDERS
Bind off 6(7:8) sts at beg of next 6 rows. *35(39:43) sts.*
Leave these sts on a spare needle.

FRONT
Work as given for back until front measures 19¾(20:20½)in/50(51:52)cm from cast-on edge, ending with a WS row.

SHAPE FRONT NECK
Next row Patt 37(40:43), turn and work on these sts for first side of neck.
Dec one st at neck edge on the next and 6 foll 4th rows. *30(33:36) sts.*
Work even until front measures the same as back to upper arm shaping, ending at side edge.

SHAPE UPPER ARM
Bind off 3 sts at beg of next and 3 foll RS rows.
Work 1 row.

SHAPE SHOULDER
Bind off 6(7:8) sts at beg of next and foll RS row.
Work 1 row.
Bind off rem 6(7:8) sts.
With RS facing, slip center 21(25:29) sts on a holder, rejoin yarn to rem sts, patt to end.
Dec one st at neck edge on the next and 7 foll 4th rows. *30(33:36) sts.*
Work even until front measures the same as back to upper arm shaping, ending at side edge.

SHAPE UPPER ARM
Bind off 3 sts at beg of next and 3 foll WS rows.
Work 1 row.

SHAPE SHOULDER
Bind off 6(7:8) sts at beg of next and foll WS row.
Work 1 row.
Bind off rem 6(7:8) sts.

SLEEVES
Using size 7 (4.5mm) needles, cast on 47(51:55) sts.
K 5 rows.
Change to size 8 (5mm) needles.
K 1 row.

Work in main patt from Chart D.
Row 1 P11(8:10), [work across 10-st patt rep]
3(4:4) times, p6(3:5).
Row 2 K6(3:5), [work across 10-st patt rep]
3(4:4) times, k11(8:10).
These 2 rows set the 20 row patt.
Work to end of row 8.
Inc and work into patt one st at each end of
the next and 16 foll 5th rows. *81(85:89) sts.*
Work even until sleeve measures 17¼in/44cm
from cast-on edge, ending with a WS row.

SHAPE TOP
Bind off 6 sts at beg of next 10 rows.
21(25:29) sts.
Bind off.

COLLAR
Join upper arm and shoulder seams.
With size 7 (4.5mm) circular needle, pick up
and k48(50:52) sts down left front neck, k
across 21(25:29) sts from front neck holder,
pick up and k49(51:53) sts up right side of
front neck, 35(39:43) sts from back neck.
153(165:177) sts.
Work in rounds.
1st round [P2, k1] to end.
Rep this round 11 times more.
Inc round [P2, k1, M1] to end.
Cont in rib as set until collar measures
4in/10cm from pick up round.
Change to size 8 (5mm) circular needle.
Work a further 4¼in/11cm.
Bind off loosely in rib.

FINISHING
With center of sleeve head to shoulder seam,
sew on sleeves. Join side and sleeve seams.

Stroll wrap

If the delicate pattern on the Stroll tunic on page 76 appeals but you fancy something a little simpler to knit, then the Stroll wrap may be the answer. Knitted in Rowan *Kid Classic*, it has the same pattern detail as the tunic, but is luxuriously wide and long, making it the perfect wrap to add interest to a plain dress.

FINISHED SIZE
ONE SIZE
14in/36cm by 81in/206cm long

YARN
Six x 1¾oz/153yd balls of Rowan *Kid Classic* in Water 883

NEEDLES
Pair each of size 7 (4.5mm) and size 8 (5mm) knitting needles
Size 9 (5.5mm) needle for binding off

GAUGE
18 sts and 25 rows to 4in/10cm square over patt using size 8 (5mm) needles, or size to obtain correct gauge.

ABBREVIATIONS
Dec 5 = k2tog tbl, k3tog, then pass k2tog tbl stitch over.
Cluster 3 = ytb, slip next 3 sts onto right-hand needle, ytf, slip same 3 sts back onto left-hand needle, ytb, then k3.
See also page 133.

FIRST SIDE
Using size 7 (4.5mm) needles, cast on 65 sts.
K 6 rows.
Change to size 8 (5mm) needles.
Work in patt from Chart.
Row 1 K3, work across 59 sts of Chart, k3.
Row 2 K3, work across 59 sts of Chart, k3.
These 2 rows set the patt with g-st border.
Work to end of row 24, then rep rows 1 to 23 again.
Cont in patt from Chart to end of row 95.
Now rep rows 76 to 95 until piece measures 40½in/103cm from cast-on edge, ending with a 90th row.
Leave these sts on a spare needle.

SECOND SIDE
Work to match first side, ending with a 91st row.
With RS together and needles pointing in the same direction, using a larger needle bind one st off from each needle together.

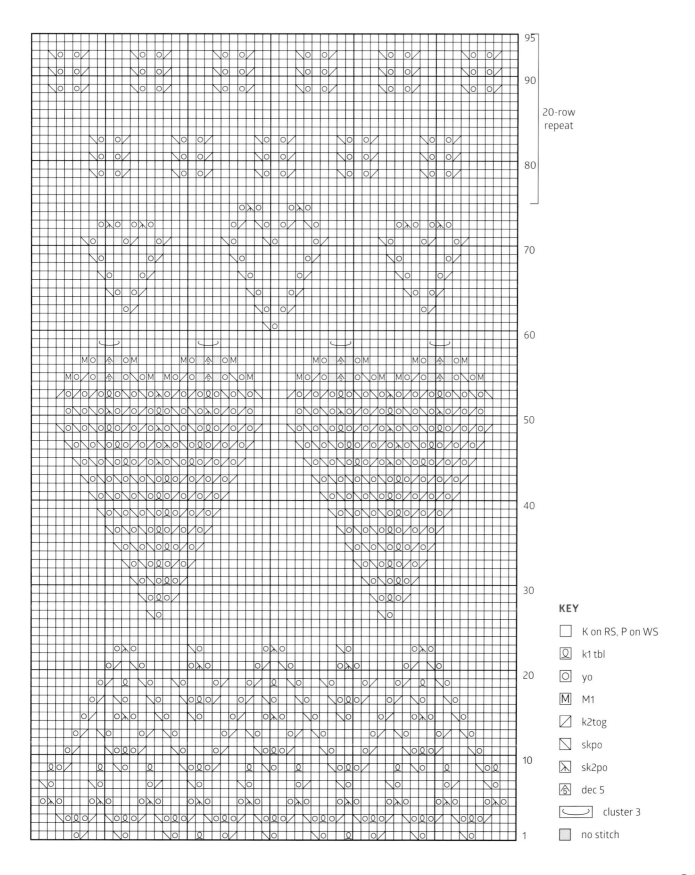

KEY

□	K on RS, P on WS
Ω	k1 tbl
O	yo
M	M1
╱	k2tog
╲	skpo
⋏	sk2po
⛋	dec 5
‿	cluster 3
▨	no stitch

Hush shrug

This is an easy shrug to wear. It is knitted in Rowan *Wool Cotton 4ply*, with a beautiful all-over textured stitch pattern that shows up really well in this soft but crisp yarn. The deep rib runs around the body of the shrug, rolling over at the front to create a flattering shawl collar.

FINISHED SIZE

To fit bust

36–38	40–42	44–46	48–50	in
92–97	102–107	112–117	122–127	cm

ACTUAL MEASUREMENTS

Width (cuff to cuff)

56	59	62	65½	in
142	150	158	166	cm

Length center back neck

23	23¼	26¾	27¼	in
58	59	68	69	cm

Sleeve length

17¾in/45cm

YARN

7(8:9:10) x 1¾oz/174yd balls of Rowan *Wool Cotton 4ply* in Sea 492

NEEDLES

Pair each of size 2 (2.75mm) and size 3 (3.25mm) knitting needles
Circular size 3 (3.25mm) needle
Cable needle
Size 6 (4mm) needle for binding off

GAUGE

28 sts and 36 rows to 4in/10cm square over patt using size 3 (3.25mm) needles, or size to obtain correct gauge.

ABBREVIATIONS

C6F = slip next 3 sts onto cable needle and hold at front of work, k3, then k3 from cable needle.
C6B = slip next 3 sts onto cable needle and hold at back of work, k3, then k3 from cable needle.
See also page 133.

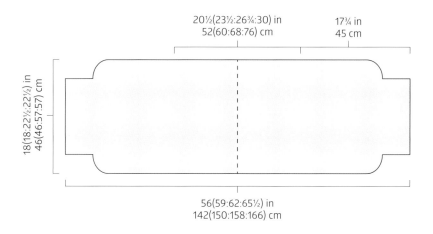

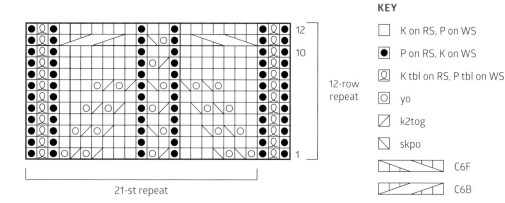

KEY

☐ K on RS, P on WS

● P on RS, K on WS

Ω K tbl on RS, P tbl on WS

○ yo

╱ k2tog

╲ skpo

⬱ C6F

⬱ C6B

12-row repeat

21-st repeat

FIRST SIDE

Using size 2 (2.75mm) needles, cast on 65(65:77:77) sts.
Row 1 P1, [k1, p1] to end.
Row 2 K1, [p1, k1] to end.
These 2 rows form the rib.
Work a further 47 rows.
1st and 2nd sizes only
Inc row Rib 1(1:-:-), [M1, p1, M1, k1] to last 0(0:-:-) sts, rib 0(0:-:-). *129(129:-:-) sts.*
3rd and 4th sizes
Inc row Rib -(-:2:2), M1, k1, [M1, p1, k1] to last -(-:2:2) sts, rib 0(0:-:-).
-(-:150:150) sts.
All sizes
Change to size 3 (3.25mm) needles.
Row 1 P1, k1tbl, p1, [work across 21-st patt rep] 6(6:7:7) times.
Row 2 [Work across 21-st patt rep] 6(6:7:7) times k1, p1tbl, k1.

These 2 rows set the 12-row patt rep.
Work even until piece measures 17¾in/45cm from cast-on edge, ending with a WS row.
Mark each end of last row with a colored thread.
Cont in patt until piece measures 28(29½:31:32¾)in/71(75:79:83)cm from cast-on edge, ending with a WS row.
Leave these sts on a spare needle.

SECOND SIDE

Work to match first side, ending with a RS row.
With RS together and needles pointing in the same direction, bind one st off from each needle together.

BORDER

Using circular size 3 (3.25mm) needle, with RS facing pick up and k150(165:180:195) sts between colored threads on one side, with WS

together fold shrug in half,
pick up and k150(165:180:195)
sts between colored
threads on second side.
300(330:360:390) sts.
Cont in rounds.
1st round K to end.
2nd round [K1, M1, k1,
p1] to end of round.
400(440:480:520) sts.
2nd round [K1, p1] to end of
round.
Rep the last round for
5(5½:6:6¼)in/13(14:15:16)cm.
Using a size 6 (4mm) needle,
bind off in rib.

FINISHING
Join sleeve seams from
colored threads to cast-on
edge.

Weekender jacket

Knitted in the self-striped Rowan *Fine Art Aran* yarn in stockinette stitch, this boxy jacket with a dropped sleeve is a short, wide design that comes just to the hip bone. It is the ideal jacket to wear for country walks with an open-necked long shirt and jeans.

FINISHED SIZE

To fit bust

36–40	42–44	46–48	in
92–102	107–112	117–122	cm

ACTUAL MEASUREMENTS

Width across back

34½	36½	38	in
88	93	97	cm

Length to shoulder

20	21¾	23¾	in
51	55	59	cm

Sleeve length

8¼in/21cm

YARN

11(12:13) x 3½oz/186yd balls of Rowan *Fine Art Aran* in Foxtrot 548

NEEDLES

Circular size 6 (4mm) and size 7 (4.5mm) needles
Pair each of size 6 (4mm) and size 7 (4.5mm) knitting needles

EXTRAS

Four big buttons

GAUGE

19 sts and 25 rows to 4in/10cm square over St st using size 7 (4.5mm) needles, or size to obtain correct gauge.

ABBREVIATIONS

Wrap 1 = ytf, sl 1, ytb, place slipped st back on left-hand needle.
See also page 133.

NOTE

When working with *Fine Art Aran*, use 2 balls at a time and work 2 rows from each ball.

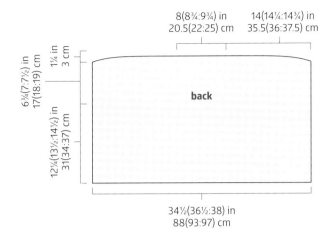

8(8¾:9¾) in
20.5(22:25) cm

14(14¼:14¾) in
35.5(36:37.5) cm

1¼ in
3 cm

6¾(7:7½) in
17(18:19) cm

back

12¼(13½:14½) in
31(34:37) cm

34½(36½:38) in
88(93:97) cm

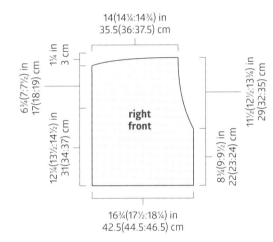

14(14¼:14¾) in
35.5(36:37.5) cm

1¼ in
3 cm

6¾(7:7½) in
17(18:19) cm

right
front

11½(12½:13¾) in
29(32:35) cm

12¼(13½:14½) in
31(34:37) cm

8¾(9:9½) in
22(23:24) cm

16¾(17½:18¼) in
42.5(44.5:46.5) cm

13½(14¼:15¼) in
34.5(36:38.5) cm

10½ in
26.5 cm

sleeve

9¾(10½:11¼) in
25(26.5:28.5) cm

BACK

Using size 6 (4mm) circular needle, cast on 170(178:186) sts.
Row 1 (RS) K2, [k2, p2] to end.
Row 2 P2, [k2, p2] to end.
These 2 rows form the rib.
Work a further 24 rows.
Change to size 7 (4.5mm) needles.
Beg with a k row, cont in St st until back measures 19(20½:22)in/48(52:56)cm from cast-on edge, ending with a p row.

SHAPE UPPER ARM

Bind off 12 sts at beg of next 8 rows.

SHAPE SHOULDERS

Bind off 9(10:11) sts at beg of next 4 rows.
Bind off rem 38(42:46) sts.

POCKET LININGS (make 2)

Using size 6 (4mm) needles, cast on 28 sts.
Beg with a k row, work 27(29:31) rows in St st.
Leave these sts on a holder.

LEFT FRONT

Using size 6 (4mm) needles, cast on 79(83:87) sts.
Row 1 (RS) K2, [p2, k2] to last 5 sts, p2, k3.
Row 2 P3, [k2, p2] to end.
These 2 rows form the rib.
Work a further 24 rows.
Change to size 7 (4.5mm) needles.
Beg with a k row, work 26(28:30) rows in St st.

PLACE POCKET LINING

Next row K to last 48(50:52) sts, k next 28 sts and place these 28 sts on a holder, k to end.
Next row P20(22:24), p across 28 sts of pocket lining, p to end.
Work 2 rows even.

SHAPE FRONT NECK

Next row K to last 4 sts, k2tog, k2.
Work 4 rows.
Next row P2, p2tog, p to end.
Work 4 rows.
These 10 rows set the front shaping.
Cont to shape as set until 13(15:17) decs have

been worked altogether at the same time when front measures the same as back to upper arm shaping, ending with a p row.

SHAPE UPPER ARM
Bind off 12 sts at beg of next and 3 foll RS rows.
Work 1 row.

SHAPE SHOULDER
Bind off 9(10:11) sts at beg of next row.
Work 1 row.
Bind off rem 9(10:11) sts.

RIGHT FRONT
Using size 6 (4mm) needles, cast on 79(83:87) sts.
Row 1 (RS) K3, [p2, k2] to end.
Row 2 P2, [k2, p2] to last 5 sts, k2, p3.
These 2 rows form the rib.
Work a further 24 rows.
Change to size 7 (4.5mm) needles.
Beg with a k row, work 26(28:30) rows in St st.

PLACE POCKET LINING
Next row K20(22:24), k next 28 sts and place these 28 sts on a holder, k to end.
Next row P31(33:35), p across 28 sts of pocket lining, p to end.
Work 2 rows even.

SHAPE FRONT NECK
Next row K2, skpo, k to end.
Work 4 rows.
Next row P to last 4 sts, p2tog tbl, p to end.
Work 4 rows.
These 10 rows set the front shaping.
Cont to shape as set until 13(15:17) decs have been worked altogether at the same time when front measures the same as back to upper arm shaping, ending with a k row.

SHAPE UPPER ARM
Bind off 12 sts at beg of next and 3 foll WS rows.
Work 1 row.

SHAPE SHOULDER
Bind off 9(10:11) sts at beg of next row.
Work 1 row.
Bind off rem 9(10:11) sts.

SLEEVES
Using size 6 (4mm) needles, cast on 46(50:54) sts.
Row 1 (RS) P2, [k2, p2] to end.
Row 2 K2, [p2, k2] to end.
These 2 rows form the rib.
Work a further 12 rows.
Change to size 7 (4.5mm) needles.
Beg with a k row, cont in St st.
Work 4 rows.
Inc row K4, M1, k to last 4 sts, M1, k4.
Work 3 rows.
Rep the last 4 rows 8 times more.
64(68:72) sts.
Bind off.

POCKET BORDERS
With RS facing, using size 6 (4mm) needles, place 28 sts for pocket front on a needle, join on yarn.
Row 1 K3, [p2, k2] to last 5 sts, p2, k3.
Row 2 K1, [p2, k2] to last 3 sts, p2, k1.
Rep these 2 rows 3 times more.
Bind off in rib.

LEFT FRONT BORDER AND COLLAR
Using size 6 (4mm) needles, cast on 19 sts.
Row 1 K9, sl 1, k9.
Row 2 P to end.
Rep the last 2 rows 27 times.

**SHAPE FOR COLLAR
Row 1 K1, M1, k to last 2 sts, M1, k1.
Row 2 P to end.
Rep the last 2 rows 31 times more. *83 sts.*
Next 2 rows K41, sl 1, k23, wrap 1, turn, p47, wrap 1, turn, k to end, working wrap together with wrapped st.
Next row P to end, working wrap together with wrapped st.
Work 2 rows across all sts.
Rep the last 4 rows until short edge fits up left front to shoulder and halfway across back neck.
Leave these sts on a holder **.

RIGHT FRONT BORDER AND COLLAR
Using size 6 (4mm) needles, cast on 19 sts.
Row 1 K9, sl 1, k9.
Row 2 P to end.
Rep the last 2 rows once more.

Buttonhole row K3, k2tog, [yo] twice, skpo, k2, sl 1, k2, k2tog, [yo] twice, skpo, k3.
Work 15 rows.
Rep the last 16 rows twice more and the buttonhole row again.
Work 3 rows.
Work as given for left front Collar from ** to **.

FINISHING

Join shoulder and upper arm seams. With RS together and needles facing same direction, bind sts from both Collars off together. Sew front band and Collar in place, fold in half lengthwise, then sew other edge in place. Sew on sleeves. Join side and sleeve seams. Sew down pocket linings and pocket borders. Sew on buttons.

Clear hat

With its simple shape and delicate beads, this is a glitzy version of the classic beanie with a softly ribbed shape. Knitted in Rowan *Wool Cotton 4ply*, it adds a touch of glamour to an outfit and will please anyone who loves to add a few beads to their knitting!

FINISHED SIZE
ONE SIZE
To fit average-sized woman's head

YARN
Two x 1¾oz/197yd balls of Rowan *Wool Cotton 4ply* in Jacaranda 502

NEEDLES
Pair each of size 2 (2.75mm) and size 3 (3.25mm) knitting needles

EXTRAS
Approx 400 small glass beads

GAUGE
28 sts and 38 rows to 4in/10cm square over patt using size 3 (3.25mm) needles, or size to obtain correct gauge.

ABBREVIATIONS
PB (place bead) = ytf, slide a bead up close to work, slip next st, ytb, so that bead lies across slipped stitch.
See also page 133.

NOTE
Thread beads onto yarn before starting to knit by threading a sewing needle with a short length of sewing cotton then knotting the ends to make a loop. Slide the knot to one side and thread yarn end through loop. Pick up beads, three or four at a time, slide them down the loop of thread and onto yarn.

TO MAKE
Using size 2 (2.75mm) needles, cast on 142 sts.
Rib row 1 P2, [k2, p2] to end.
Rib row 2 K2, [p2, k2] to end.
Rep the last 2 rows 4 times more and the first row again.
Inc row (WS) Rib 3, [M1, rib 4] to last 3 sts, M1, rib 3. *177 sts.*
Change to size 3 (3.25mm) needles and patt.
Row 1 P1, k1, [k3, p1, k1] to end.
Row 2 K1, p1, [p3, k1, p1] to end.
Row 3 P1, k1, [k1, pb, k1, p1, k1] to end.

Row 4 K1, p1, [p3, k1, p1] to end.

Row 5 P1, k1, [k3, p1, k1] to end.

Row 6 K1, p1, [p3, k1, p1] to end.

These 6 rows form the patt. Work even until hat measures 6¼in/16cm from cast-on edge, ending with row 6.

SHAPE CROWN

Row 1 P1, k1, [k3, p2tog] to end. *142 sts.*

Row 2 P to end.

Row 3 P1, k1, [k1, PB, k1, p1] to end.

Row 4 P to end.

Row 5 P1, k1, [k3, p1] to end.

Row 6 P to end.

Row 7 P1, [k2tog, k2] to last st, p1. *107 sts.*

Row 8 P to end.

Row 9 P1, [k1, PB, k1] to last st, p1.

Row 10 P to end.

Row 11 P1, k to last st, p1.

Row 12 P to end.

Row 13 K2tog, [k1, k2tog] to last 3 sts, k3. *72 sts.*

Row 14 P to end.

Row 15 [K1, PB] to last 2 sts, k2.

Row 16 P to end.

Row 17 K1, [k2tog] to last st, k1. *37 sts.*

Row 18 P to end.

Row 19 K1, [k2tog] to end. *19 sts.*

Row 20 P1, [p2tog] to end. *10 sts.*

Leaving a long end, cut off yarn and thread through rem sts.

FINISHING

Join seam.

Clear fingerless gloves

And here are the long fingerless gloves to match the hat! Knitted in the same yarn and softly ribbed stitch, they are also similarly beaded. Like the hat, they can be worn to dress up a plain outfit and add some glitz!

FINISHED SIZE
ONE SIZE
To fit average-sized woman's hand

YARN
Two × 1¾oz/197yd balls of Rowan *Wool Cotton 4ply* in Jacaranda 502

NEEDLES
Pair each of size 2 (2.75mm), size 2–3 (3mm), and size 3 (3.25mm) knitting needles

EXTRAS
Approx 470 small glass beads

GAUGE
28 sts and 38 rows to 4in/10cm square over patt using size 3 (3.25mm) needles, or size to obtain correct gauge.

ABBREVIATIONS
PB (place bead) = ytf, slide a bead up close to work, slip next st, ytb, so that bead lies across slipped stitch.
See also page 133.

NOTE
Thread beads onto yarn before starting to knit by threading a sewing needle with a short length of sewing cotton then knotting the ends to make a loop. Slide the knot to one side and thread yarn end through loop. Pick up beads, three or four at a time, slide them down the loop of thread and onto yarn.

TO MAKE
Using size 3 (3.25mm) needles, cast on 82 sts.
Rib row 1 P2, [k3, p2] to end.
Rib row 2 K2, [p3, k2] to end.
Rep the last 2 rows 4 times more.
Work in patt.
Row 1 P1, k1, [k3, p1, k1] to end.
Row 2 K1, p1, [p3, k1, p1] to end.
Row 3 P1, k1, [k1, PB, k1, p1, k1] to end.
Row 4 K1, p1, [p3, k1, p1] to end.
Row 5 P1, k1, [k3, p1, k1] to end.
Row 6 K1, p1, [p3, k1, p1] to end.
These 6 rows form the patt.

Work even until glove measures 3½in/9cm from cast-on edge, ending with row 6.
Change to size 2–3 (3mm) needles.
Work even until glove measures 7in/18cm from cast-on edge, ending with row 6.
Dec row P1, k1, [k3, p2tog] to last 5 sts, k3, p1, k1. *67 sts.*
Next row K1, p to last 2 sts, k1, p1.
Next row P1, k1, [k1, PB, k1, p1] to last 5 sts, k1, PB, k1, p1, k1.
Next row P to end.
Next row P1, k1, [k3, p1] to last 5 sts, k3, p1, k1.
Next row P to end.
Next row P1, k1, [k3, p1] to last 5 sts, k3, p1, k1.
Rep the last 6 rows until glove measures 9½in/24cm from cast-on edge, ending with a WS row.
Change to size 2 (2.75mm) needles.
Work even until glove measures 11in/28cm from cast-on edge, ending with a WS row.
Rib row 1 P2, [k3, p1] to last st, p1.
Rib row 2 K2, [p3, k1] to last st, k1.
Rep the last 2 rows twice more.
Bind off in rib.

FINISHING
Leaving an opening for thumb, join seam.

Shingle cardigan

This is a very flattering, softly shaped raglan-sleeved cardigan knitted in the self-striped Rowan *Alpaca Colour*. The low neck and gently fluted shape of the cardigan is easy to wear regardless of figure shape, the three buttons just catch the front and allow the lower part of the cardigan to open softly to reveal the top or dress underneath.

FINISHED SIZE

To fit bust

36	38	40	42	44	46	in
92	97	102	107	112	117	cm

ACTUAL MEASUREMENTS

Bust

39½	41¼	43¾	45½	48	50	in
100	105	111	116	122	127	cm

Length to back neck

25	25½	26½	26¾	27	27½	in
64	65	67	68	69	70	cm

Sleeve length

17¾in/45cm

YARN

11(12:13:14:15:16) x 1¾oz/131yd balls of Rowan *Alpaca Colour* in Garnet 139

NEEDLES

Circular size 6 (4mm) and size 5 (3.75mm) needles
Pair each of size 5 (3.75mm) and size 6 (4mm) knitting needles

EXTRAS

3 buttons

GAUGE

22 sts and 28 rows to 4in/10cm square over St st using size 6 (4mm) needles, or size to obtain correct gauge.

ABBREVIATIONS

See page 133.

BACK

Using size 6 (4mm) circular needle, cast on 168(174:180:186:192:198) sts.
1st row K14, [p8, k14(15:16:17:18:19)] 6 times, p8, k14.
2nd row P14, [k8, p14(15:16:17:18:19)] 6 times, k8, p14.
These 2 rows set the rib.
Work a further 10 rows.
1st dec row K14, [p3, p2tog, p3, k14(15:16:17:18:19)] 6 times, p3, p2tog, p3, k14. *161(167:173:179:185:191) sts.*
Work a further 11 rows.

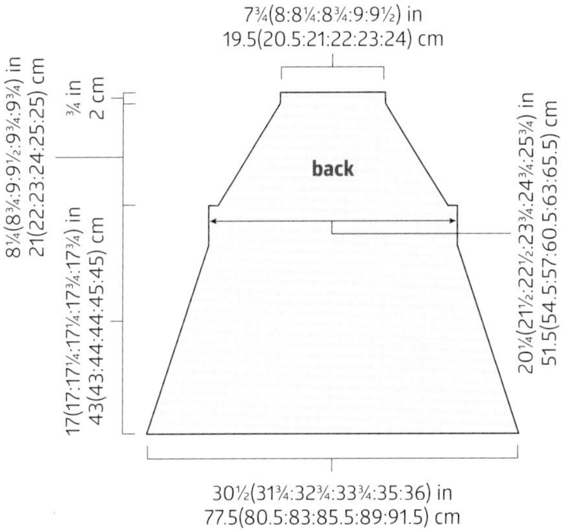
7¾(8:8¼:8¾:9:9½) in
19.5(20.5:21:22:23:24) cm
back
¾ in
2 cm
8¼(8¾:9:9½:9¾:9¾) in
21(22:23:24:25:25) cm
17(17:17¼:17¼:17¾:17¾) in
43(43:44:44:45:45) cm
20¼(21½:22½:23¾:24¾:25¾) in
51.5(54.5:57:60.5:63:65.5) cm
30½(31¾:32¾:33¾:35:36) in
77.5(80.5:83:85.5:89:91.5) cm

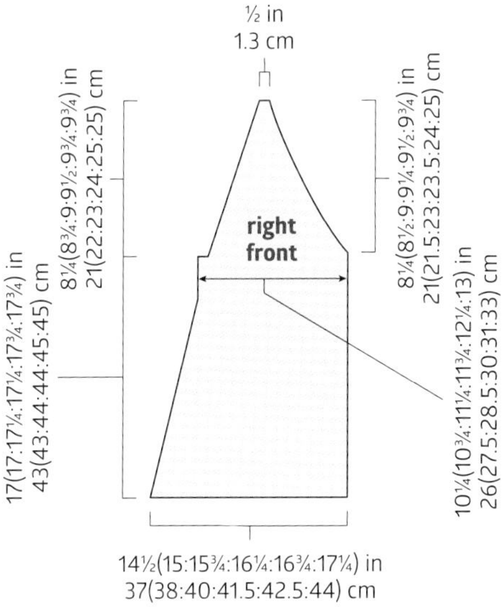
½ in
1.3 cm
right front
8¼(8¾:9:9½:9¾:9¾) in
21(22:23:24:25:25) cm
17(17:17¼:17¼:17¾:17¾) in
43(43:44:44:45:45) cm
8¼(8½:9:9¼:9½:9¾) in
21(21.5:23:23.5:24:25) cm
10¼(10¾:11¼:11¾:12¼:13) in
26(27.5:28.5:30:31:33) cm
14½(15:15¾:16¼:16¾:17¼) in
37(38:40:41.5:42.5:44) cm

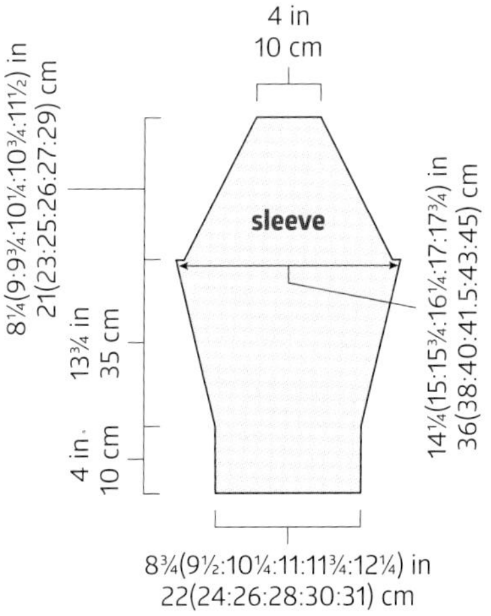
4 in
10 cm
sleeve
8¼(9:9¾:10¼:10¾:11½) in
21(23:25:26:27:29) cm
13¾ in
35 cm
4 in
10 cm
14¼(15:15¾:16¼:17:17¾) in
36(38:40:41.5:43:45) cm
8¾(9½:10¼:11:11¾:12¼) in
22(24:26:28:30:31) cm

2nd dec row K14, [p2, p2tog, p3, k14(15:16:17:18:1)9] 6 times, p2, p2tog, p3, k14. *154(160:166:172:178:184) sts.*
Work a further 11 rows.
3rd dec row K14, [p2, p2tog, p2, k14(15:16:17:18:19)] 6 times, p2, p2tog, p2, k14. *147(153:159:165:171:177) sts.*
Work a further 11 rows.
4th dec row K14, [p1, p2tog, p2, k14(15:16:17:18:19)] 6 times, p1, p2tog, p2, k14. *140(146:152:158:164:170) sts.*
Work a further 11 rows.
5th dec row K14, [p1, p2tog, p1, k14(15:16:17:18:19)] 6 times, p1, p2tog, p1, k14. *133(139:145:151:157:163) sts.*
Work a further 11 rows.
6th dec row K14, [p2tog, p1, k14(15:16:17:18:19)] 6 times, p2tog, p1, k14. *126(132:138:144:150:156) sts.*
Work a further 11 rows.
7th dec row K14, [p2tog, k14(15:16:17:18:19)] 6 times, p2tog, k14.
119(125:131:137:143:149) sts.
Work a further 11 rows.
8th dec row K14, [k2tog, k13(14:15:16:17:18)] 6 times, k2tog, k13.
112(118:124:130:136:142) sts.
Beg with a p row, cont in St st until back measures 17(17:17¼:17¼:17¾:17¾) in/43(43:44:44:45:45)cm from cast-on edge, ending with a p row.

SHAPE RAGLAN ARMHOLES

Bind off 6(7:8:9:10:11) sts at beg of next 2 rows. *100(104:108:112:116:120) sts.*
Next row K2, skpo, k to last 4 sts, k2tog, k2.
Next row P to end.
Rep the last 2 rows 28(29:30:31:32:33) times more. *42(44:46:48:50:52) sts.*
Change to size 5 (3.75mm) needles.
K 11 rows.
Bind off.

LEFT FRONT

Using size 6 (4mm) needles, cast on 80(83:86:89:92:95) sts.
1st row K14, [p8, k14(15:16:17:18:19)] 3 times.
2nd row [P14(15:16:17:18:19), k8] 3 times, p14.
These 2 rows set the rib.
Work a further 10 rows.
1st dec row K14, [p3, p2tog, p3,

k14(15:16:17:18:19)] 3 times.
77(80:83:86:89:92) sts.
Work a further 11 rows.
2nd dec row K14, [p2, p2tog, p3, k14(15:16:17:18:19)] 3 times.
74(77:80:83:86:89) sts.
Work a further 11 rows.
3rd dec row K14, [p2, p2tog, p2, k14(15:16:17:18:19)] 3 times.
71(74:77:80:83:86) sts.
Work a further 11 rows.
4th dec row K14, [p1, p2tog, p2, k14(15:16:17:18:19)] 3 times.
68(71:74:77:80:83) sts.
Work a further 11 rows.
5th dec row K14, [p1, p2tog, p1, k14(15:16:17:18:19)] 3 times.
65(68:71:74:77:80) sts.
Work a further 11 rows.
6th dec row K14, [p2tog, p1, k14(15:16:17:18:19)] 3 times.
62(65:68:71:74:77) sts.
Work a further 11 rows.
7th dec row K14, [p2tog, k14(15:16:17:18:19)] 3 times. *59(62:65:68:71:74) sts.*
Work a further 11 rows.
8th dec row K14, [k2tog, k13(14:15:16:17:18)] 3 times. *56(59:62:65:68:71) sts.*
Beg with a p row, cont in St st until front measures 17(17:17¼:17¼:17¾:17¾)in/ 43(43:44:44:45:45)cm from cast-on edge, ending with a p row.

SHAPE RAGLAN ARMHOLE
Next row Bind off 6(7:8:9:10:11) sts, k to end. *50(52:54:56:58:60) sts.*
Next row P to end.
Next row K2, skpo, k to last 4 sts, k2tog, k2.
Next row P to end.
Rep the last 2 rows 17(18:19:20:21:22) times more.
Next row K2, skpo, k to end.
Next row P to end.
Rep the last 2 rows 10 times more. *3 sts.*
Leave these 3 sts on a holder.

RIGHT FRONT
Using size 6 (4mm) needles, cast on 80(83:86:89:92:95) sts.
1st row [K14(15:16:17:18:19), p8] 3 times, k14.

2nd row P14, [k8, p14(15:16:17:18:19)] 3 times.
These 2 rows set the rib.
Work a further 10 rows.
1st dec row [K14(15:16:17:18:19), p3, p2tog, p3] 3 times, k14. *77(80:83:86:89:92) sts.*
Work a further 11 rows.
2nd dec row [K14(15:16:17:18:19), p2, p2tog, p3] 3 times, k14. *74(77:80:83:86:89) sts.*
Work a further 11 rows.
3rd dec row [K14(15:16:17:18:19), p2, p2tog, p2] 3 times, k14. *71(74:77:80:83:86) sts.*
Work a further 11 rows.
4th dec row [K14(15:16:17:18:19), p2, p2tog, p1] 3 times, k14. *68(71:74:77:80:83) sts.*
Work a further 11 rows.
5th dec row [K14(15:16:17:18:19), p1, p2tog, p1] 3 times, k14. *65(68:71:74:77:80) sts.*
Work a further 11 rows.
6th dec row [K14(15:16:17:18:19), p2tog, p1] 3 times, k14. *62(65:68:71:74:77) sts.*
Work a further 11 rows.
7th dec row [K14(15:16:17:18:19), p2tog] 3 times, k14. *59(62:65:68:71:74) sts.*
Work a further 11 rows.
8th dec row K14, k2tog, [k13(14:15:16:17:18), k2tog] twice, k13. *56(59:62:65:68:71) sts.*
Beg with a p row, cont in St st until front measures 17(17:17¼:17¼:17¾:17¾)in/ 43(43:44:44:45:45)cm from cast-on edge, ending with a k row.

SHAPE RAGLAN ARMHOLE
Next row Bind off 6(7:8:9:10:11) sts, p to end. *50(52:54:56:58:60) sts.*
Next row K2, skpo, k to last 4 sts, k2tog, k2.
Next row P to end.
Rep the last 2 rows 17(18:19:20:21:22) times more.
Next row K to last 4 sts, k2tog, k2.
Next row P to end.
Rep the last 2 rows 10 times more. *3 sts.*
Leave these 3 sts on a holder.

SLEEVES
Using size 5 (3.75mm) needles, cast on 48(52:56:60:64:68) sts.
K 1 row.
Beg with a k row, work 28 rows in St st.
Change to size 6 (4mm) needles.
Work 2 rows.

Inc row K3, M1, k to last 3 sts, M1, k3.
Work 5 rows.
Rep the last 6 rows 13 times more and the inc
row again. *78(82:86:90:94:98) sts.*
Cont even until Sleeve measures 17¾in/45cm
from cast-on edge, ending with a p row.

SHAPE RAGLAN TOP
Bind off 6(7:8:9:10:11) sts at beg of next 2
rows. *66(68:70:72:74:76) sts.*
Next row K2, skpo, k to last 4 sts, k2tog, k2.
Next row P to end.
Next row K to end.
Next row P to end.
Rep the last 4 rows 6 times more.
52(54:56:58:60:62) sts.
Next row K2, skpo, k to last 4 sts, k2tog, k2.
Next row P to end.
Rep the last 2 rows 14(15:16:17:18:19) times
more. *22 sts.*
Leave these sts on a spare needle.

RIGHT FRONT BAND
With RS facing, using size 5 (3.75mm) circular
needle, pick up and k86(86:89:89:92:92) sts to
beg of neck shaping, 51(53:53:55:55:57) sts
along neck edge, k2 from holder, k last st tog
with first st on right sleeve, k21.
K 5 rows.
Buttonhole row 1 K60(60:61:61:62:62), [bind
off 4 sts, k6(6:7:7:8:8) inc st used to bind
off] twice, bind off 4, k to **end.**
Buttonhole row 2 K to end, casting on 4 sts
over those bound off in previous row.
K 4 rows.
Bind off.

LEFT FRONT BAND
With RS facing, using size 5 (3.75mm) circular
needle, k21 sts from left sleeve, k last st
tog with first st on left front holder, k2,
pick up and k51(53:53:55:55:57) sts to beg of
neck shaping, k86(86:89:89:92:92) sts to cast-
on edge.
K 11 rows.
Bind off.

FINISHING
Join raglan seams. Join side and sleeve seams.
Sew on buttons.

Pacific slipover

This great slipover is ideal for layering over a top. The low, softly rolled collar is flattering to the face. It finishes on the hip and looks great worn with pants or a softly flared skirt. The big all-over cable pattern adds interest both in terms of the design and in the knitting. It is knitted in Rowan *Pure Wool 4ply*.

FINISHED SIZE

To fit bust

36–40	42–44	46–48	in
92–102	107–112	117–122	cm

ACTUAL MEASUREMENTS

Bust

40	44	49	in
102	112	124	cm

Length to shoulder

24	24¾	25½	in
61	63.5	66	cm

YARN

12(13:14) x 1¾oz/174yd balls of Rowan *Pure Wool 4ply* in Blue Iris 455

NEEDLES

Pair each of size 2–3 (3mm) and size 3 (3.25mm) knitting needles
Cable needle
Stitch holder

GAUGE

32 sts and 41 rows to 4in/10cm square over patt using size 3 (3.25mm) needles, or size to obtain correct gauge.

ABBREVIATIONS

C6B = slip next 3 sts onto cable needle and hold at back of work, k3, then k3 from cable needle.
C6F = slip next 3 sts onto cable needle and hold at front of work, k3, then k3 from cable needle.
C8B = slip next 4 sts onto cable needle and hold at back of work, k4, then k4 from cable needle.
C8F = slip next 4 sts onto cable needle and hold at front of work, k4, then k4 from cable needle.
See also page 133.

NOTE

When working from Chart, right side rows read from right to left and wrong side rows read from left to right.

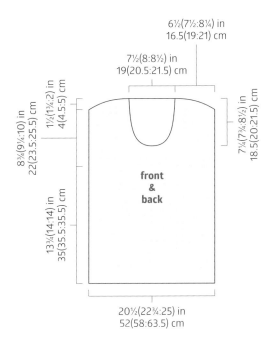

6½(7½:8¼) in
16.5(19:21) cm

7½(8:8½) in
19(20.5:21.5) cm

1½(1¾:2) in
4(4.5:5) cm

8¾(9¼:10) in
22(23.5:25.5) cm

7¼(7¾:8½) in
18.5(20:21.5) cm

13¾(14:14) in
35(35.5:35.5) cm

**front
&
back**

20½(22¾:25) in
52(58:63.5) cm

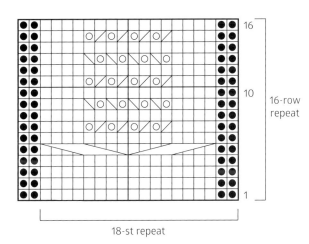

16

10

1

16-row
repeat

18-st repeat

KEY

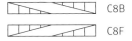

☐ K on RS, P on WS

⬛ P on RS, K on WS

▢ yo

◰ k2tog

◲ skpo

▱ C8B

▱ C8F

BACK
Using size 3 (3.25mm) circular needle, cast on 164(182:200) sts.
Row 1 (RS) P2, [k6, p4, k6, p2] 9(10:11) times.
Row 2 K2, [p6, k4, p6, k2] 9(10:11) times.
Row 3 P2, [C6B, p4, C6F, p2] 9(10:11) times.
Row 4 K2, [p6, k4, p6, k2] 9(10:11) times.
These 4 rows form the cable rib.
Work a further 20 rows.
Work in main patt.
Row 1 (RS) P2, [work across 18-st patt rep] 9(10:11) times.
Row 2 [Work across 18-st patt rep] 9(10:11) times, k2.
These 2 rows set the patt.
Cont in patt until back measures 22½(23¾:24)in/ 57(59:61)cm from cast-on edge, ending with a WS row.

SHAPE UPPER ARM
Bind off 5 sts at beg of next 16(18:20) rows. *84(92:100) sts.*

SHAPE SHOULDERS
Bind off 12(14:16) sts at beg of next 2 rows.
Leave rem 60(64:68) sts on a spare needle.

FRONT
Work as given for Back until front measures 17(17¼:17¾)in/43(44:45)cm from cast-on edge, ending with a WS row.

SHAPE NECK
Next row Patt 67(74:81), turn and work on these sts for first side of neck shaping.
Dec one st at neck edge on every RS row until 52(59:66) sts rem.
Work even until front measures the same as back to upper arm shaping, ending at side edge.

SHAPE UPPER ARM
Bind off 5 sts at beg of next and 7(8:9) foll RS rows. *12(14:16) sts.*
Work 1 row.

SHAPE SHOULDER
Bind off rem 12(14:16) sts.
With RS facing, place center 30(34:38) sts on a holder, rejoin yarn to rem sts, patt to end.
Dec one st at neck edge on every RS row until 52(59:66) sts rem.

Work even until front measures the same as back to upper arm shaping, ending at side edge.

SHAPE UPPER ARM
Bind off 5 sts at beg of next and 7(8:9) foll WS rows. *12(14:16) sts.*
Work 1 row.

SHAPE SHOULDER
Bind off rem 12(14:16) sts.

COLLAR
Join right upper sleeve and shoulder seam. Using size 2–3 (3mm) circular needle, pick up and k64(66:68) sts down left front neck, k across 30(34:38) sts from front neck holder, pick up and k64(66:68) sts up RS of front neck, k60(64:68) sts from back neck. *218(230:242) sts.*
1st rib row K2, [p2, k2] to end.
2nd rib row P2, [k2, p2] to end.
Rep the last 2 rows until collar measures 5½in/14cm.
Change to size 3 (3.25mm) circular needle.
Work a further 7in/18cm.
Bind off loosely in rib.

SLEEVE BANDS
Join left upper sleeve and shoulder seam and collar, reversing seam on last 8in/20cm.
Place a marker 90(96:102) rows down from shoulder seam on back and front.
With RS facing, using size 2–3 (3mm) circular needle, pick up and k134(142:150) sts between markers.
Beg with p2, work in p2, k2 rib.
Next 2 rows Rib to last 40 sts, turn.
Next 2 rows Rib to last 36 sts, turn.
Next 2 rows Rib to last 32 sts, turn.
Next 2 rows Rib to last 28 sts, turn.
Cont in this way working 4 extra sts on every row until 8 sts are left unworked at each end.
Next row Rib to end.
Work a further 12 rows.
Bind off in rib.

FINISHING
Join side and sleeve band seams.

Rest cardigan

Another good cable design, this time for a short-sleeved cardigan with an optional tie belt, it is knitted in Rowan *Pure Wool 4ply*. The cardigan has a ribbed shawl collar and cap sleeves. It can dress up to be worn with a shirt and skirt but looks equally good with jeans and a t-shirt.

FINISHED SIZE

To fit bust

36–40	42–44	46–48	in
92–102	107–112	117–122	cm

ACTUAL MEASUREMENTS

Bust

39½	44	49	in
100	112	124	cm

Length to shoulder

24¾	25½	26¾	in
63	65	68	cm

YARN

10(11:12) x 1¾oz/197yd balls of Rowan *Pure Wool 4ply* in Eau de Nil 450

NEEDLES

Pair each of size 2–3 (3mm) and size 3 (3.25mm) knitting needles
Circular size 2–3 (3mm) needle
Cable needle

GAUGE

32 sts and 41 rows to 4in/10cm square over patt using size 3 (3.25mm) needles, or size to obtain correct gauge.

ABBREVIATIONS

C4B = slip next 2 sts onto cable needle and hold at back of work, k2, then k2 from cable needle.
C4F = slip next 2 sts onto cable needle and hold at front of work, k2, then k2 from cable needle.
See also page 133.

BACK

Using size 3 (3.25mm) needles, cast on 162(182:202) sts.
Row 1 (RS) P2, [work across 10-st patt rep] 16(18:20) times.
Row 2 [Work across 10-st patt rep] 16(18:20) times, k2.
These 2 rows set the patt.
Cont in patt until back measures 23¼(24:24¾) in/59(61:63)cm from cast-on edge, ending with a WS row.

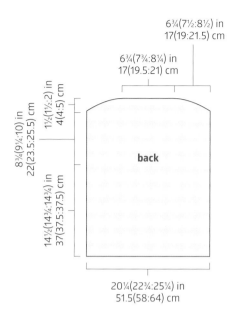

6¾(7½:8½) in
17(19:21.5) cm

6¾(7¾:8¼) in
17(19.5:21) cm

1½(1½:2) in
4(4:5) cm

8¾(9¼:10) in
22(23.5:25.5) cm

14½(14¾:14¾) in
37(37.5:37.5) cm

back

20¼(22¾:25¼) in
51.5(58:64) cm

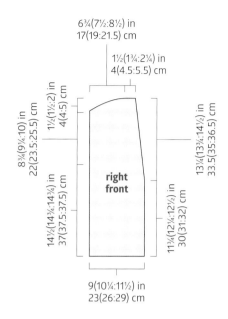

6¾(7½:8½) in
17(19:21.5) cm

1½(1¾:2¼) in
4(4.5:5.5) cm

1½(1½:2) in
4(4:5) cm

8¾(9¼:10) in
22(23.5:25.5) cm

14½(14¾:14¾) in
37(37.5:37.5) cm

right
front

13¼(13¾:14½) in
33.5(35:36.5) cm

11¾(12¼:12½) in
30(31:32) cm

9(10¼:11½) in
23(26:29) cm

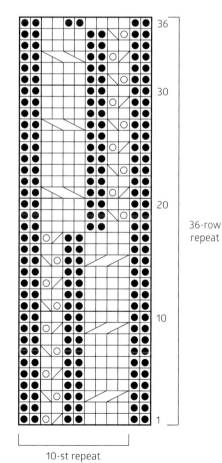

36-row
repeat

10-st repeat

KEY

☐ K on RS, P on WS

⬤ P on RS, K on WS

◎ yo

◺ k2tog

◹ skpo

⬛ C4B

⬛ C4F

SHAPE UPPER ARMS
Bind off 5 sts at beg of next 16(18:20) rows. *82(92:102) sts.*

SHAPE SHOULDERS
Bind off 13(15:17) sts at beg of next 2 rows.
Bind off rem 56(62:68) sts.

LEFT FRONT
Using size 3 (3.25mm) needles, cast on 72(82:92) sts.
Row 1 (RS) P2, [work across 10-st patt rep] 7(8:9) times.
Row 2 [Work across 10-st patt rep] 7(8:9) times, k2.
These 2 rows set the patt.
Cont in patt until front measures 11¾(12¼:12½) in/30(31:32)cm from cast-on edge, ending with a WS row.

SHAPE FRONT NECK
Next row Patt to last 2 sts, work 2 tog.
Patt 3 rows.
Rep the last 4 rows until 53(60:67) sts rem.
Work even until front measures the same as back to upper arm shaping, ending at side edge.

SHAPE UPPER ARM
Bind off 5 sts at beg of next and 7(8:9) foll RS rows. *13(15:17) sts.*
Work 1 row.

SHAPE SHOULDER
Bind off rem 13(15:17) sts.

RIGHT FRONT
Using size 3 (3.25mm) needles, cast on 72(82:92) sts.
Row 1 (RS) P2, [work across 10-st patt rep] 7(8:9) times.
Row 2 [Work across 10-st patt rep] 7(8:9) times, k2.
These 2 rows set the patt.
Cont in patt until front measures 11¾(12¼:12½) in/30(31:32)cm from cast-on edge, ending with a WS row.

SHAPE FRONT NECK
Next row Work 2 tog, patt to end.
Patt 3 rows.
Rep the last 4 rows until 53(60:67) sts rem.

Work even until front measures the same as back to upper arm shaping, ending at side edge.

SHAPE UPPER ARM
Bind off 5 sts at beg of next and 7(8:9) foll WS rows. *13(15:17) sts.*
Work 1 row.

SHAPE SHOULDER
Bind off rem 13(15:17) sts.

LEFT NECK EDGE and COLLAR
With RS facing, using size 2–3 (3mm) circular needle, cast on 29(32:35) sts, pick up and k92(94:96) sts down neck edge to beg of neck shaping, 85(88:91) sts to cast-on edge. *206(214:222) sts.*
Row 1 (WS) P2, [k2, p2] to end.
This row sets the rib.

SHAPE FOR COLLAR
Next 2 rows Rib 34(38:42), turn, rib to end.
Next 2 rows Rib 42(46:50), turn, rib to end.
Next 2 rows Rib 50(54:58), turn, rib to end.
Next 2 rows Rib 58(62:66), turn, rib to end.
Cont in this way working 8 more sts on every RS row until 122(126:130) sts have been worked into collar, ending with a WS row.
Work 27(29:31) rows across all sts.
Bind off in rib.

RIGHT NECK EDGE and COLLAR
With RS facing, using size 2–3 (3mm) circular needle, pick up and k85(88:91) sts to beg of neck shaping, 92(94:96) sts up neck edge to shoulder, cast on 29(32:35) sts. *206(214:222) sts.*
Next 2 rows P2, [k2, p2] 8(9:10) times, turn, rib to end.
These 2 rows set the rib.

SHAPE FOR COLLAR
Next 2 rows Rib 42(46:50), turn, rib to end.
Next 2 rows Rib 50(54:58), turn, rib to end.
Next 2 rows Rib 58(62:66), turn, rib to end.
Cont in this way working 8 more sts on every WS row until 122(126:130) sts have been worked into collar, ending with a RS row.
Work 28(30:32) rows across all sts.
Bind off in rib.

SLEEVE BANDS

Join upper sleeve and shoulder seams.
Place a marker 90(96:102) rows down from
shoulder seam on back and front.
With RS facing, using size 2-3 (3mm) circular
needle, pick up and k134(142:150) sts between
markers.
Beg with p2, work in p2, k2 rib.
Next 2 rows Rib to last 40 sts, turn.
Next 2 rows Rib to last 36 sts, turn.
Next 2 rows Rib to last 32 sts, turn.
Next 2 rows Rib to last 30 sts, turn.
Cont in this way working 4 extra sts on every
row until 10 sts are left unworked at each
end.
Next row Rib to end.
Work a further 12 rows.
Bind off in rib.

BELT

Using size 3 (3.25mm) needles, cast on 16 sts.
Row 1 K3, p2, [k2, p2] twice, k3.
Row 2 K1, [p2, k2] 3 times, p2, k1.
These 2 rows form the rib.
Cont in rib until belt measures 59in/150cm or
length required.
Bind off in rib.

FINISHING

Join back seam of Collar, sew to back neck.
Join side and underarm seams.

Tranquil shrug

A little shrug, this time with a pretty trellis stitch pattern, knitted in Rowan *Wool Cotton 4 ply*. It comes to just below the bust and the short sleeves provide useful cover over a sleeveless top or dress.

FINISHED SIZE

To fit bust

36–38	40–42	44–46	48–50	in
92–97	102–107	112–117	122–127	cm

ACTUAL MEASUREMENTS

Width (cuff to cuff)

30	33	36¼	39½	in
76	84	92	100	cm

Length center back neck

19	19	20½	20½	in
48	48	52	52	cm

Sleeve length

3½in/9cm

YARN

5(6:8:9) x 1¾oz/197yd balls of Rowan *Wool Cotton 4ply* in Flower 485

NEEDLES

Pair each of size 2 (2.75mm) and size 3 (3.25mm) needles
Circular size 3 (3.25mm) needle
Cable needle
Size 6 (4mm) needle for binding off

GAUGE

28 sts and 36 rows to 4in/10cm square over St st using size 3 (3.25mm) needles, or size to obtain correct gauge.

ABBREVIATIONS

SB (Small bobble) = [k1, p1, k1] all into next st, turn, p3, turn, sk2po.
C4F = slip next 2 sts onto cable needle and hold at front of work, k2, then k2 from cable needle.
C3R = slip next st onto cable needle and hold at back of work, k2, then p1 from cable needle.
C3L = slip next 2 sts onto cable needle and hold at front of work, p1, then k2 from cable needle.
See also page 133.

NOTE

When working from Chart, right side rows read from right to left and wrong side rows from left to right.

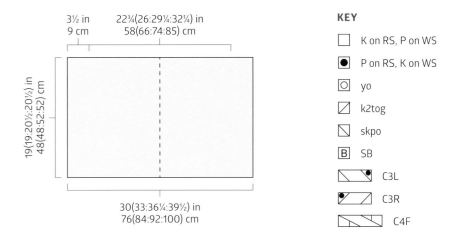

KEY

☐ K on RS, P on WS

⬛ P on RS, K on WS

⊙ yo

⧄ k2tog

⧅ skpo

B SB

C3L

C3R

C4F

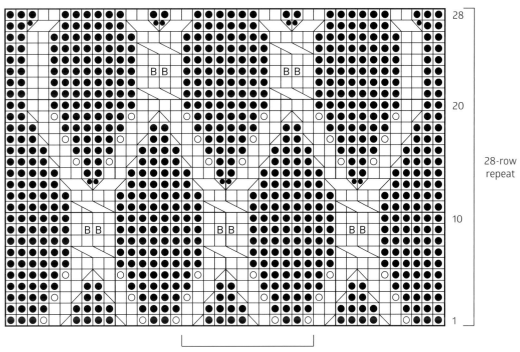

28

20

10

1

28-row
repeat

12-st repeat

FIRST SIDE

Using size 2 (2.75mm) needles, cast on 100(100:112:112) sts.
K 5 rows.
Change to size 3 (3.25mm) needles.
Work from Chart.
Row 1 Work first 12 sts, [work across 12-st patt rep] 6(6:7:7) times, work across last 16 sts of Chart.
Row 2 Work first 16 sts, [work across 12-st patt rep] 6(6:7:7) times, work across last 12 sts of Chart.
These 2 rows set the Chart.
Work a further 26 rows.
Mark each end of last row with a colored thread.
Cont in patt until piece measures approx 15(16½:18:19½)in/38(42:46:50)cm from cast-on edge, ending with a 23rd(9th:23rd:9th) patt row.
Leave these sts on a spare needle.

SECOND SIDE

Work to match first side, ending with a 22nd(8th:22nd:8th) patt row.
With RS together and needles pointing in the same direction, bind one st off from each needle together.

BORDER

Using circular size 3 (3.25mm) needle, with RS facing, pick up and k186(201:216:231) sts between colored threads on one side, with WS together fold shrug in half, pick up and k186(201:216:231) sts between colored threads on second side. *372(402:432:462) sts.*
Cont in rounds.
1st round [K1, p2] to end of round.
2nd round [K1, M1, p2] to end of round. *496(536:576:616) sts.*
3rd round [K2, p2] to end of round.
Rep the last round for 5(5½:6:6¼)in/13(14:15:16)cm.
Using a size 6 (4mm) needle, bind off in rib.

FINISHING

Join sleeve seams from colored threads to cast-on edge.

Calm sweater

This very simple sweater, knitted in stockinette stitch in Rowan *Kid Classic*, has a scooped neck and three quarter sleeves. The sleeve cuffs and the rib at the hem are worked in a contrast color, picking up one of the colors in the flower design on the front. You can work the flower design as colorwork or, if you prefer, you could knit the front plain and duplicate stitch the flower design onto it using the chart.

FINISHED SIZE

To fit bust

36	38	40	42	44	46	in
92	97	102	107	112	117	cm

ACTUAL MEASUREMENTS

Bust

39¾	42	44½	47¼	49½	52	in
101	107	113	120	126	132	cm

Length to back neck

25	25½	26	26½	26¾	27	in
64	65	66	67	68	69	cm

Sleeve length

10¼in/26cm

YARNS

Rowan *Kid Classic*
6(6:7:7:8:8) x 1¾oz/153yd balls in Royal 835 (A)
2(2:2:3:3:3) x 1¾oz/153yd balls in Tea Rose 854 (B)
Small amounts of Grasshopper 886, Lime 882, Victoria 852, Water 883, and Nightly 846

NEEDLES

Pair each of size 6 (4mm) and size 8 (5mm) knitting needles
Stitch holder

GAUGE

19 sts and 25 rows to 4in/10cm square over St st using size 8 (5mm) needles, or size to obtain correct gauge.

ABBREVIATIONS

See page 133.

NOTE

When working from Chart, use the Fairisle and Intarsia method.
The motif can also be duplicate stitched after the front has been worked. If you wish to duplicate stitch the design, you simply embroider two small straight stitches over each "V" of the stockinette stitch pattern in the yarn colors shown in the chart.

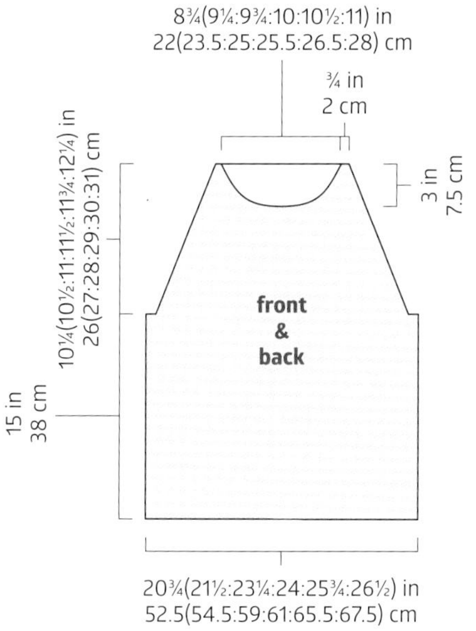
8¾(9¼:9¾:10:10½:11) in
22(23.5:25:25.5:26.5:28) cm
¾ in
2 cm
10¼(10½:11:11½:11¾:12¼) in
26(27:28:29:30:31) cm
3 in
7.5 cm
front
&
back
15 in
38 cm
20¾(21½:23¼:24:25¾:26½) in
52.5(54.5:59:61:65.5:67.5) cm

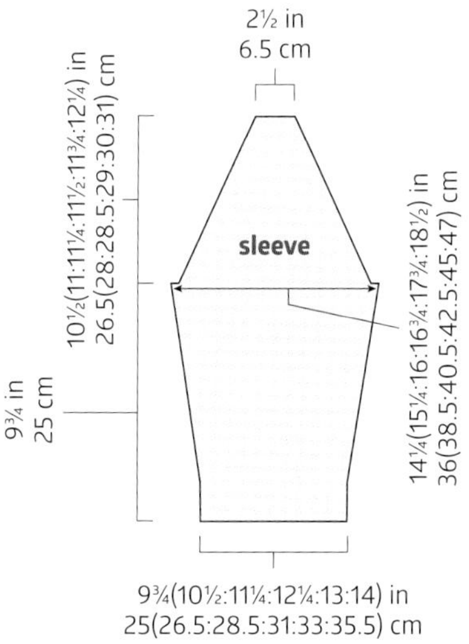
2½ in
6.5 cm
10½(11:11¼:11½:11¾:12¼) in
26.5(28:28.5:29:30:31) cm
sleeve
14¼(15¼:16:16¾:17¾:18½) in
36(38.5:40.5:42.5:45:47) cm
9¾ in
25 cm
9¾(10½:11¼:12¼:13:14) in
25(26.5:28.5:31:33:35.5) cm

BACK

Using size 6 (4mm) needles and B, cast on 98(102:110:114:122:126) sts.

1st rib row K3, [yo, skpo, k2] to last 3 sts, yo, skpo, k1.

2nd rib row P3, [yo, p2tog, p2] to last 3 sts, yo, p2tog, p1.

These 2 rows form the faggoted rib patt.

Work a further 22 rows.

Break off B.

Join on A.

Change to size 8 (5mm) needles.

Beg with a k row and inc 2 sts evenly across row on 2nd, 4th, and 6th sizes only, cont in St st. *98(104:110:116:122:128) sts.*

Work even until Back measures 15in/38cm from cast-on edge, ending with a p row.

SHAPE RAGLAN ARMHOLES

Bind off 3(4:5:6:7:8) sts at beg of next 2 rows. *92(96:100:104:108:112) sts.*

Next row K2, skpo, k to last 4 sts, k2tog, k2.

Next row P to end.

Next row K to end.

Next row P to end.

Rep the last 4 rows 10 times more. *70(74:78:82:86:90) sts.*

Next row K2, skpo, k to last 4 sts, k2tog, k2.

Next row P to end.

Rep the last 2 rows 10(11:12:13:14:15) times more. *48(50:52:54:56:58) sts.*

Leave these sts on a spare needle.

FRONT

Work as given for Back until 10(10:12:12:14:14) rows fewer have been worked than on Back to armhole shaping.

Place Chart

1st row K24(27:30:33:36:39)A, work across 1st row of Chart, k25(28:31:34:37:40)A.

2nd row P25(28:31:34:37:40)A, work across 2nd row of Chart, p24(27:30:33:36:39)A.

These 2 rows set the Chart.

Work a further 8(8:10:10:12:12) rows.

SHAPE RAGLAN ARMHOLES

Bind off 3(4:5:6:7:8) sts at beg of next 2 rows. *92(96:100:104:108:112) sts.*

Next row K2, skpo, k to last 4 sts, k2tog, k2.

Next row P to end.

Next row K to end.

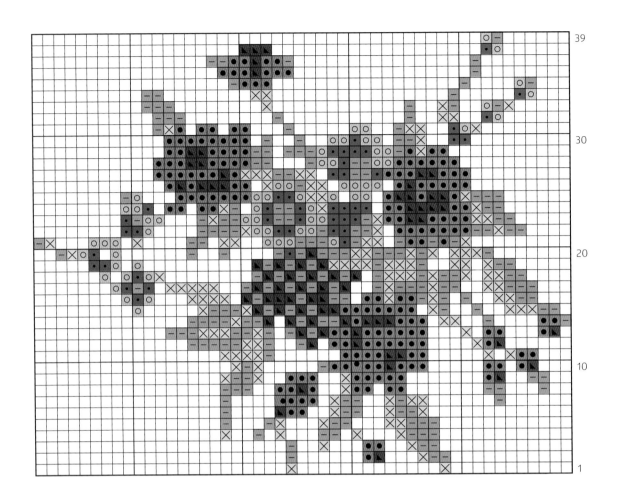

Next row P to end.
Rep the last 4 rows 9 times more.
72(76:80:84:88:92) sts.
Next row K2, skpo, k to last 4 sts, k2tog, k2.
Next row P to end.
Rep the last 2 rows 3(4:5:6:7:8) times more.
64(66:68:70:72:74) sts.

SHAPE FRONT NECK
Next row K2, skpo, k21, turn, and work on
these sts for first side of neck shaping.
Next row Bind off 2 sts, p to end.
Next row K2, skpo, k to end.
Rep the last 2 rows 6 times more.
Next row P to end. *3 sts.*
Leave these 3 sts on a holder.
With RS facing, place center
14(16:18:20:22:24) sts on a holder, rejoin
yarn to rem sts, k to last 4 sts, k2tog, k2.
24 sts.
Next row P to end.

Next row Bind off 2 sts, k to last 4 sts,
k2tog, k2.
Rep the last 2 rows 6 times more.
Next row P to end. *3 sts.*
Leave these 3 sts on a holder.

Key

☐ Royal 835 (A)

▣ Nightly 846

⬤ Tea Rose 854 (B)

⊟ Grasshopper 886

⊠ Lime 882

◣ Victoria 852

⊙ Water 883

SLEEVES

Using size 6 (4mm) needles and B, cast on
46(50:54:58:62:66) sts.
1st rib row K3, [yo, skpo, k2] to last 3 sts,
yo, skpo, k1.
2nd rib row P3, [yo, p2tog, p2] to last 3 sts,
yo, p2tog, p1.
These 2 rows form the faggoted rib patt.
Work a further 16 rows.
Break off B.
Join on A.
Change to size 8 (5mm) needles.
Beg with a k row, cont in St st.
Work 2 rows.
Inc row K3, M1, k to last 3 sts, M1, k3.
Work 3 rows.
Rep the last 4 rows 10 times more.
68(72:76:80:84:88) sts.

SHAPE RAGLAN ARMHOLES

Bind off 3(4:5:6:7:8) sts at beg of next 2
rows. *62(64:66:68:70:72) sts.*
Next row K2, skpo, k to last 4 sts, k2tog, k2.
Next row P to end.
Next row K to end.
Next row P to end.
Rep the last 4 rows 6 times more.
48(50:52:54:56:58) sts.
Next row K2, skpo, k to last 4 sts, k2tog, k2.
Next row P to end.
Rep the last 2 rows 17(18:19:20:21:22) times
more. *12 sts.*
Leave these sts on a spare needle.

NECKBAND

With RS facing, using size 6 (4mm) needles
and A, k11, from left sleeve, k last st
tog with first st on left front holder, k2,
pick up and k14 sts down left side of front
neck, k14(16:18:20:22:24) sts on front neck
holder, pick up and k14 sts up right side of
front neck, k2, k last st on front tog with
first st on right sleeve, k10, k last st tog
with first st on back, k47(49:51:53:55:57).
117(121:125:129:133:137) sts.
K 4 rows.
Bind off.

FINISHING

Join raglan seams. Join side and sleeve seams.

Relax wrap

Knitted in the subtly self-striped Rowan *Fine Art*, this lovely design has a relatively simple filigree lace pattern worked all over it. The yarn, which is a wool/silk/mohair/polyamide blend, shows up the lace pattern beautifully and is light yet warm.

FINISHED SIZE
ONE SIZE
18½in/47cm by 71in/180cm long

YARN
Four x 3½oz/437yd hanks of Rowan *Fine Art* in Hornbeam 311

NEEDLES
Pair of size 3 (3.25mm) knitting needles

GAUGE
32 sts and 44 rows to 4in/10cm square over Chart A using size 3 (3.25mm) needles, or size to obtain correct gauge.

ABBREVIATIONS
Cluster 3 = ytb, slip next 3 sts onto right-hand needle, ytf, slip same 3 sts back onto left-hand needle, ytb, then k3.
Dec 5 = k2tog tbl, k3tog, then pass k2tog stitch over.
cdi (center double increase) = [k1tbl, k1] into next st, then insert left-hand needle point behind the vertical strand that runs downward from between the 2 sts just made and k1tbl into this strand to make 3rd stitch of the group. See also page 133.

NOTE
When working from Chart, right side rows read from right to left and wrong side rows from left to right.

FIRST SIDE
Using size 3 (3.25mm) needles, cast on 150 sts.
Work from Chart A.
Row 1 K3, [work across 18-st patt rep] 8 times, k3.
Row 2 K3, [work across 18-st patt rep] 8 times, k3.
These 2 rows set the 4-row patt rep.
Work a further 37 rows, ending row 3.
Row 40 K3, inc 3 sts evenly, p to last 3 sts, k3. *153 sts.*
Work from Chart B.
Row 1 K3, [work across 16-st patt rep] 9 times, k6.

Chart A

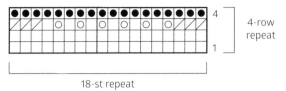

4-row
repeat

18-st repeat

Chart B

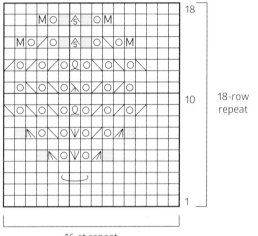

18-row
repeat

16-st repeat

KEY

☐	K on RS, P on WS
●	P on RS, K on WS
Ⓠ	k1 tbl
Ⓞ	yo
Ⓥ	cdi
Ⓜ	M1
⟋	k2tog
⟍	skpo
⟑	sk2po
⟋	k3tog
⟍	k3tog tbl
⟑	dec 5
⌣	cluster 3
☐	no stitch

Row 2 K3, p3, [work across 16-st patt rep] 9 times, k3.
These 2 rows set the patt.
Cont in patt to end of row 18.
Rep rows 1 to 18 until piece measures approx 35½in/90cm from cast-on edge, ending with row 2.
Leave these sts on a spare needle.

SECOND SIDE
Work to match first side, ending with a row 1.
With RS together and needles pointing in the same direction, [k one st together from each needle] twice, * bind off first st, then k one st together from each needle; rep from * until all sts have been bound off.

Coast coat

This terrific cable coat is a great winter staple, and the yarn (Rowan *Wool Cotton*) is crisp enough to show up the texture to perfection. A longer length design, it makes a versatile cover-up, stylish yet casual. You can wear it edge to edge or fasten it with a kilt pin at the bust, if you prefer.

FINISHED SIZE

To fit bust

36-40	42-46	in
92-102	107-117	cm

ACTUAL MEASUREMENTS

Bust

55	66	in
140	168	cm

Length to shoulder

28¾	29½	in
73	75	cm

Sleeve length

12in/30cm

YARN

29(34) x 1¾oz/123yd balls of Rowan *Wool Cotton* in Smalt 963

NEEDLES

Circular size 3 (3.25mm) and size 5 (3.75mm) needles
Cable needle

GAUGE

24 sts and 32 rows to 4in/10cm square over St st using size 5 (3.75mm) needles, or size to obtain correct gauge.

ABBREVIATIONS

C6B = slip next 3 sts onto cable needle and hold at back of work, k3, then k3 from cable needle.
C6F = slip next 2 sts onto cable needle and hold at front of work, k2, then k2 from cable needle.
C5R = slip next 2 sts onto cable needle and hold at back of work, k3, then p2 from cable needle.
C5L = slip next 3 sts onto cable needle and hold at front of work, p2, then k3 from cable needle.
See also page 133.

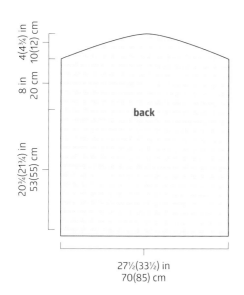

8 in / 20 cm

4(4¾) in / 10(12) cm

20¾(21¾) in / 53(55) cm

back

27½(33½) in / 70(85) cm

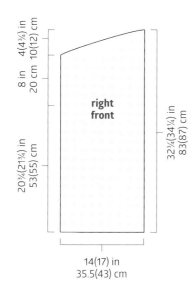

8 in / 20 cm

4(4¾) in / 10(12) cm

20¾(21¾) in / 53(55) cm

32¾(34¼) in / 83(87) cm

right front

14(17) in / 35.5(43) cm

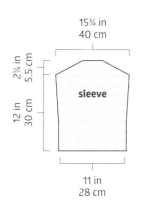

15¾ in / 40 cm

2¼ in / 5.5 cm

12 in / 30 cm

sleeve

11 in / 28 cm

NOTE

When working from Chart, right side rows read from right to left and wrong side rows read from left to right.

For Panel A: Work rows 1 to 42, then rep rows 27 to 42.

For Panel B: Work rows 1 to 46, then rep rows 31 to 46.

For Panel C: Work rows 1 to 50, then rep rows 27 to 50.

BACK

Using size 3 (3.25mm) circular needle, cast on 235(285) sts.

Row 1 P3, k1, work across row 1 of [Panel A, k1] 1(2) time(s), Panel B, k1, Panel C, k1, Panel B, k1, Panel B, k1, Panel C, k1, Panel B, [k1, Panel A] 1(2) time(s), k1, p3.

Row 2 K3, p1, work across row 2 of [Panel A, p1] 1(2) time(s), Panel B, p1, Panel C, p1, Panel B, p1, Panel B, p1, Panel C, p1, Panel B, [p1, Panel A] 1(2) time(s), p1, k3.

These 2 rows set the Panels.

Work to the end of row 24.

Change to size 5 (3.75mm) circular needle.

Row 25 K1, p1, k2, work across row 25 of [Panel A, k1] 1(2) time(s), Panel B, k1, Panel C, k1, Panel B, k1, Panel B, k1, Panel C, k1, Panel B, [k1, Panel A] 1(2) time(s), k2, p1, k1.

Row 26 [K1, p1] twice, work across row 26 of [Panel A, p1] 1(2) time(s), Panel B, p1, Panel C, p1, Panel B, p1, Panel B, p1, Panel C, p1, Panel B, [p1, Panel A] 1(2) time(s), [p1, k1] twice.

These 2 rows set the Panels, with seed st edgings.

Work even until back measures 28¾(29½)in/ 73(75)cm from cast-on edge, ending with a WS row.

SHAPE SHOULDERS

Bind off 7 sts at beg of next 6 rows then 8 sts at beg of next 24(30) rows.

1(3) st(s) rem.

Bind off.

Panel A

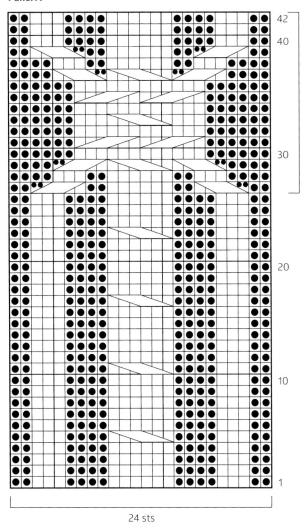

42
40

16-row
repeat

30

20

10

1

24 sts

Panel B

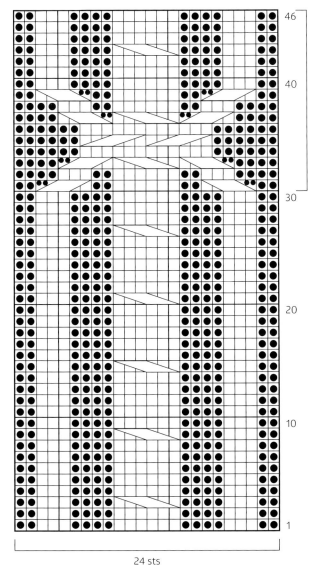

46

40

16-ro
repea

30

20

10

1

24 sts

KEY

☐ K on RS, P on WS

▣ P on RS, K on WS

C5R

C5L

C6B

C6F

Panel C

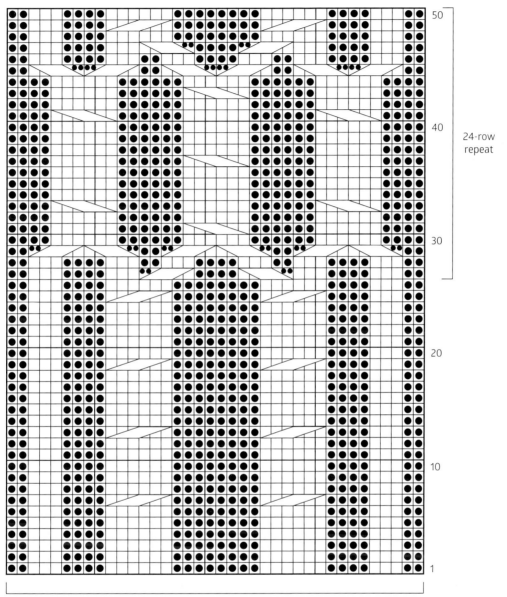

38 sts

LEFT FRONT

With size 3 (3.25mm) circular needle, cast on 119(144) sts.

Row 1 P3, k1, work across row 1 of [Panel A, k1] 1(2) time(s), Panel B, k1, Panel C, k1, Panel B, k1, p1.

Row 2 K1, p1, work across row 2 of Panel B, p1, Panel C, p1, Panel B, [p1, Panel A] 1(2) time(s), p1, k3.

These 2 rows set the Panels.

Work to the end of row 24.

Change to size 5 (3.75mm) circular needle.

Row 25 K1, p1, k2, work across row 25 of [Panel A, k1] 1(2) time(s), Panel B, k1, Panel C, k1, Panel B, k1, p1.

Row 26 K1, p1, work across row 26 of Panel B, p1, Panel C, p1, Panel B, [p1, Panel A] 1(2) time(s), [p1, k1] twice.

These 2 rows set the Panels, with seed st edging at side edge.

Work even until front measures the same as back to shoulder, ending at armhole edge.

SHAPE SHOULDER

Bind off 7 sts at beg of next and 2 foll RS rows then 8 sts at beg of next 12 RS rows. 2(3) sts rem.

Work 2(3) tog and fasten off.

RIGHT FRONT

Using size 3 (3.25mm) circular needle, cast on 119 sts.

Row 1 P1, k1, work across row 1 of Panel B, k1, Panel C, k1, Panel B, [k1, Panel A] 1(2) time(s), k1, p3.

Row 2 K3, p1, work across row 2 of [Panel A, p1] 1(2) time(s), Panel B, p1, Panel C, p1, Panel B, p1, k1.

These 2 rows set the Panels.

Work to the end of row 24.

Change to size 5 (3.75mm) circular needle.

Row 25 P1, k1, work across row 25 of Panel B, k1, Panel C, k1, Panel B, [k1, Panel A] 1(2) time(s), k2, p1, k1.

Row 26 [K1, p1] twice, work across row 26 of [Panel A, p1] 1(2) time(s), Panel B, p1, Panel C, p1, Panel B, p1, k1.

These 2 rows set the Panels, with seed st edging at side edge.

Work even until front measures the same as back to shoulder, ending at armhole edge.

SHAPE SHOULDER

Bind off 7 sts at beg of next and 2 foll WS rows then 8 sts at beg of next 12(15) WS rows. 2(3) sts rem.

Work 2(3) tog and fasten off.

SLEEVES

Using size 3 (3.25mm) circular needle, cast on 120 sts.

Row 1 P4, k4, p4, [k6, p4, k4, p4] to end.

Row 2 K4, p4, k4, [p6, k4, p4, k4] to end.

Rows 3 and 4 As rows 1 and 2.

Row 5 P4, k4, p4, [C6B, p4, k4, p4] to end.

Row 6 As row 2.

These 6 rows form the cable patt.

Work a further 24 rows.

Change to size 5 (3.75mm) circular needle.

Cont in patt until sleeve measures 12in/30cm from cast-on edge, ending with a WS row.

Bind off 6 sts at beg of next 16 rows.

24 sts.

Bind off.

LEFT FRONT BAND

With RS facing, size 3 (3.25mm) circular needle, pick up and k186(190) sts evenly along left front edge.

1st row P2, [k2, p2] to end.

2nd row K2, [p2, k2] to end.

These 2 rows form the rib.

Work a further 25 rows.

Bind off in rib.

RIGHT FRONT BAND

With RS facing, size 3 (3.25mm) circular needle, pick up and k186(190) sts evenly along right front edge.

1st row P2, [k2, p2] to end.

2nd row K2, [p2, k2] to end.

These 2 rows form the rib.

Work a further 25 rows.

Bind off in rib.

FINISHING

Join shoulder seams. Join front band seam. Sew on sleeves. Join side and sleeve seams.

Peace wrap

With its delicate little lacy design, this gossamer-like wrap in Rowan *Kidsilk Haze* is ethereally light yet warm. Without any shaping, it is a great lace pattern for anyone wanting to try their hand at a more textured design. It would work very well, too, in a scaled down version, both narrower and shorter, to brighten up a formal suit, for example.

FINISHED SIZE
ONE SIZE
13½in/34cm by 67in/170cm long

YARN
Four x 1oz/229yd balls of Rowan *Kidsilk Haze* in Cream 634

NEEDLES
Pair of size 3 (3.25mm) knitting needles
Cable needle
Size 6 (4mm) needle for binding off

GAUGE
28 sts and 36 rows to 4in/10cm square over St st using size 3 (3.25mm) needles, or size to obtain correct gauge.

ABBREVIATIONS
MB (make bobble) = [k1, p1, k1] all into next st, turn, p3, turn, sk2po.
C4B = slip next 2 sts onto cable needle and hold at back of work, k2, then k2 from cable needle.
See also page 133.

NOTE
When working from Chart, right side rows read from right to left and wrong side rows from left to right.

FIRST SIDE
Using size 3 (3.25mm) needles, cast on 91 sts.
Row 1 [Work across 15-st patt rep] 6 times, k1.
Row 2 P1, [work across 15-st patt rep] 6 times.
These 2 rows set the patt panel.
Work even until piece measures 33½in/85cm from cast-on edge, ending with a 10th row.
Leave these sts on a spare needle.

SECOND SIDE
Work to match first side, ending with an 11th row.
With RS together and needles pointing in the same direction, using a larger needle bind one st off from each needle together.

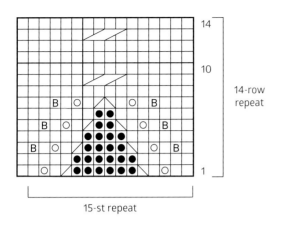

15-st repeat

14-row repeat

KEY

☐	K on RS, P on WS
●	P on RS, K on WS
⊙	yo
◹	k2tog
◺	skpo
B	MB
⬚⬚	C4B

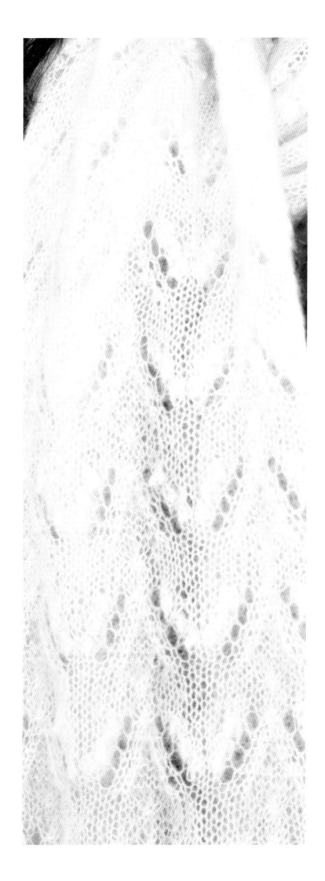

Serene cardigan

A lovely cardigan in luxuriously soft Rowan *Kid Classic*, the simple shape is emphasized with the contrasting border for the hem, cuff, collar, and button bands. The lower neckline is flattering, as is the embroidered detail on the collar. The raglan sleeves leave plenty of room to layer t-shirts underneath.

FINISHED SIZE
To fit bust

36	38	40	42	44	46	in
92	97	102	107	112	117	cm

ACTUAL MEASUREMENTS
Bust

40	42½	44¾	47½	50	52½	in
102	108	114	121	127	133	cm

Length to back neck

21½	22	22½	22¾	22¾	23¼	in
55	56	57	58	58	59	cm

Sleeve length
13¼in/34cm

YARNS
6(7:7:8:8:9) x 1¾oz/153yd balls of Rowan *Kid Classic* in Tea Rose 854 (M)
Two x 1¾oz/153yd balls in Grasshopper 886 (C)
Small amounts in contrast colors for embroidery

NEEDLES
Circular size 6 (4mm) and size 8 (5mm) needles
Pair each of size 6 (4mm) and size 8 (5mm) knitting needles
Tapestry needle
Stitch holders

EXTRAS
5 buttons

GAUGE
19 sts and 25 rows to 4in/10cm square over St st using size 8 (5mm) needles, or size to obtain correct gauge.

ABBREVIATIONS
See page 133.

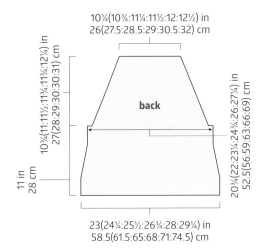

10¼(10¾:11¼:11½:12:12½) in
26(27.5:28.5:29:30.5:32) cm

10¾(11:11½:11¾:11¾:12¼) in
27(28:29:30:30:31) cm

back

20¾(22:23¼:24¾:26:27¼) in
52.5(56:59:63:66:69) cm

11 in
28 cm

23(24¼:25½:26¾:28:29¼) in
58.5(61.5:65:68:71:74.5) cm

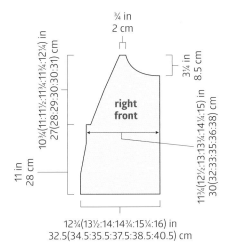

¾ in
2 cm

10¾(11:11½:11¾:11¾:12¼) in
27(28:29:30:30:31) cm

3¼ in
8.5 cm

right
front

11¾(12½:13:13¾:14¼:15) in
30(32:33:35:36:38) cm

11 in
28 cm

12¾(13½:14:14¾:15¼:16) in
32.5(34.5:35.5:37.5:38.5:40.5) cm

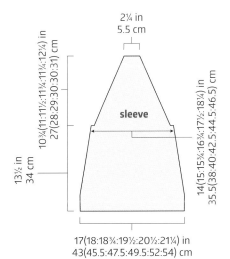

2¼ in
5.5 cm

10¾(11:11½:11¾:11¾:12¼) in
27(28:29:30:30:31) cm

sleeve

14(15:15¾:16¾:17½:18¼) in
35.5(38:40:42.5:44.5:46.5) cm

13½ in
34 cm

17(18:18¾:19½:20½:21¼) in
43(45.5:47.5:49.5:52:54) cm

BACK

Using size 6 (4mm) circular needle and C, cast on 109(115:121:127:133:139) sts.

Seed st row K1, [p1, k1] to end.

This row forms the seed st, work a further 9 rows.

Break off C.

Join on M.

Change to size 8 (5mm) needles.

Beg with a k row, cont in St st.

Work 10 rows.

Dec row K8, skpo, k to last 10 sts, k2tog, k8.

Work 9 rows.

Rep the last 10 rows 3 times more and the dec row again. *99(105:111:117:123:129) sts.*

Work even until Back measures 11in/28cm from cast-on edge, ending with a p row.

SHAPE RAGLAN ARMHOLES

Bind off 3(4:5:6:7:8) sts at beg of next 2 rows. *93(97:101:105:109:113) sts.*

Next row K2, skpo, k to last 4 sts, k2tog, k2.

Next row P to end.

Next row K to end.

Next row P to end.

Rep the last 4 rows 10 times more. *71(75:79:83:87:91) sts.*

Next row K2, skpo, k to last 4 sts, k2tog, k2.

Next row P to end.

Rep the last 2 rows 10(11:12:13:14:15) times more. *49(51:53:55:57:59) sts.*

Bind off.

LEFT FRONT

Using size 6 (4mm) needles and C, cast on 61(64:67:70:73:76) sts.

1st, 3rd, and 5th sizes only

Seed st row K1, [p1, k1] to end.

This row forms the seed st, work a further 9 rows.

2nd, 4th, and 6th sizes only

1st row [K1, p1] to end.

2nd row [P1, k1] to end.

These 2 rows form the seed st.

Work a further 8 rows.

All sizes

Break off C.

Join on M.

Change to size 8 (5mm) needles.

1st row Using M, k54(57:60:63:66:69), join on C, seed st 7.

2nd row Using C, seed st 7, using M, p to end.
These 2 rows form the St st with seed st border in C.
Work 8 rows.
Dec row K8, skpo, patt to end.
Work 9 rows.
Rep the last 10 rows 3 times more and the dec row again.
56(59:62:65:68:71) sts.
Work even until Front measures 11in/28cm from cast-on edge, ending with a WS row.

SHAPE RAGLAN ARMHOLE
Next row Bind off 3(4:5:6:7:8) sts, patt to end. *53(55:57:59:61:63) sts.*
Next row Patt to end.
Next row K2, skpo, patt to end.
Next row Patt to end.
Next row Patt to end.
Next row Patt to end.
Rep the last 4 rows 10 times more.
42(44:46:48:50:52) sts.
Next row K2, skpo, patt to end.
Next row Patt to end.
Rep the last 2 rows 0(1:2:3:4:5) time(s) more.
41(42:43:44:45:46) sts.

SHAPE FRONT NECK
Next row K2, skpo, k24, turn and work on these sts for first side of neck shaping, place rem 13(14:15:16:17:18) sts on a holder.
Next row Bind off 2 sts, p to end.
Next row K2, skpo, k to end.
Rep the last 2 rows 6 times more. *6 sts.*
Next row P to end.
Next row K2, skpo, k to end.
Rep the last 2 rows once more.
Next row P to end.
Leave these 4 sts on a holder.
Mark position for buttons, the first 4 rows below neck shaping, 4 more spaced at 2¾in/7cm apart.

RIGHT FRONT
Work buttonholes to match markers as folls:
Buttonhole row (RS) Using C, seed st 2, work 2 tog, yo, seed st 3, using M, k to end.
Using size 6 (4mm) needles and C, cast on 61(64:67:70:73:76) sts.
1st, 3rd, and 5th sizes only
Seed st row K1, [p1, k1] to end.

This row forms the seed st, work a further 9 rows.
2nd, 4th, and 6th sizes only
1st row [P1, k1] to end.
2nd row [K1, p1] to end.
These 2 rows form the seed st.
Work a further 8 rows.
All sizes
Change to size 8 (5mm) needles.
1st row Using C, seed st 7, using M, k to end.
2nd row Using M, p54(57:60:63:66:69), using C, seed st 7.
These 2 rows form the St st with seed st border in C.
Work 8 rows.
Dec row Patt to last 10 sts, k2tog, k8.
Work 9 rows.
Rep the last 10 rows 3 times more and the dec row again. *56(59:62:65:68:71) sts.*
Work even until Front measures 11in/28cm from cast-on edge, ending with a RS row.

SHAPE RAGLAN ARMHOLE
Next row Bind off 3(4:5:6:7:8) sts, patt to end. *53(55:57:59:61:63) sts.*
Next row Patt to last 4 sts, k2tog, k2.
Next row Patt to end.
Next row Patt to end.
Next row Patt to end.
Rep the last 4 rows 10 times more.
42(44:46:48:50:52) sts.
Next row Patt to last 4 sts, k2tog, k2.
Next row Patt to end.
Rep the last 2 rows 0(1:2:3:4:5) time(s) more.
41(42:43:44:45:46) sts.

SHAPE FRONT NECK
Next row Patt 13(14:15:16:17:18), leave these sts on a holder, k to last 4 sts, k2tog, k2.
27 sts.
Next row P to end.
Next row Bind off 2 sts, k to last 4 sts, k2tog, k2.
Rep the last 2 rows 6 times more. *6 sts.*
Next row P to end.
Next row K to last 4 sts, k2tog, k2.
Rep the last 2 rows once more.
Next row P to end.
Leave these 4 sts on a holder.

SLEEVES

Using size 6 (4mm) needles and C, cast on 81(85:89:93:97:101) sts.

Seed st row K1, [p1, k1] to end.

This row forms the seed st, work a further 9 rows.

Break off C.

Join on M.

Change to size 8 (5mm) needles.

Beg with a k row, cont in St st.

Work 4 rows.

Dec row K8, skpo, k to last 10 sts, k2tog, k8.

Work 9 rows.

Rep the last 10 rows 5 times more and the dec row again.

Work even until sleeve measures 13¼in/34cm from cast-on edge, ending with a WS row.

SHAPE RAGLAN ARMHOLES

Bind off 3(4:5:6:7:8) sts at beg of next 2 rows. *61(63:65:67:69:71) sts.*

Next row K2, skpo, k to last 4 sts, k2tog, k2.

Next row P to end.

Next row K to end.

Next row P to end.

Rep the last 4 rows 6 times more. *47(49:51:53:55:57) sts.*

Next row K2, skpo, k to last 4 sts, k2tog, k2.

Next row P to end.

Rep the last 2 rows 18(19:20:21:22:23) times more. *11 sts.*

Leave these sts on a spare needle.

COLLAR

With RS facing, using size 6 (4mm) circular needle, place 13(14:15:16:17:18) sts from right front on a needle, join in M, pick up and k20 sts up right side of front, k3, k next st tog with first st on sleeve, k8, k2tog, pick up and k47(49:51:53:55:57) sts from back neck, k2tog, k8, k last st on sleeve tog with first st on front, k3, pick up and k20 sts down left side of front neck, patt 13(14:15:16:17:18) sts from left front.

139(143:147:151:155:159) sts.

Work in St st in M and seed st borders in C.

Row 1 Using C, bind off 4 sts, seed st next 2 sts, using M, k96(99:102:105:108:111) sts, turn.

Row 2 P67(69:71:73:75:77), turn.

Row 3 K73(75:77:79:81:83), turn.

Row 4 P79(81:83:85:87:89), turn.

Row 5 K85(87:89:91:93:95), turn.

Row 6 P91(93:95:97:99:101), turn.

Row 7 K97(99:101:103:105:107), turn.

Row 8 P103(105:107:109:111:113), turn.

Row 9 K109(111:113:115:117:119), turn.

Row 10 P115(117:119:121:123:125), turn.

Row 11 K to last 7 sts, using C, seed st 7.

Row 12 Using C, bind off 4 sts, seed st next 2 sts, using M, p to last 3 sts, using C, seed st 3.

Change to size 8 (5mm) circular needle.

Next row Using C, seed st 3 sts, using M, k2, M1, k to last 5 sts, M1, k2, using C, seed st 3.

Work 3 rows.

Rep the last 4 rows 5 times more.

Cont in C only.

Next row Seed st 3, k to last 3 sts, seed st.

Work 3 rows in seed st across all sts.

Bind off in seed st.

FINISHING

Join raglan seams. Join side and sleeve seams. Work embroidery as shown. Sew on buttons.

EMBROIDERY

The embroidery on the collar is worked in wool yarn. I did this embroidery freehand, as I like the slightly irregular look.

The flower petals and center are worked in satin stitch, the leaves and stems are worked in chain stitches.

Chain stitch leaves and stem

Bring the yarn from the back of the work to the front, loop the yarn, using your forefinger to hold it place, and insert the needle tip back into the work over the looped yarn. Pull the needle and yarn through. Make the next stitch in the chain the same way.

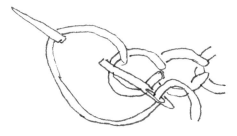

Satin stitch petals

Fill in the area with straight stitches, worked next to each other without a gap. In the flower here, the stitches were worked from the center toward the outside edge of the petals, filling in each petal in turn.

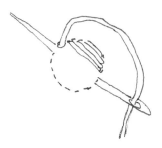

Satin stitch flower center

Fill in with satin stitch and then work a couple of darker contrasting stitches for the "eye."

Useful information

SIZING

The instructions are given for the smallest size, and larger sizes follow in parentheses. If there is only one set of figures, it refers to all sizes. If - (hyphen) or 0 (zero) is given in an instruction for the size you are knitting, then that particular instruction does not apply to your size.

Included with each garment pattern in this book is a size diagram of the finished garment pieces and their dimensions. The size diagram shows the finished width of the garment at the underarm point, and it is this measurement that you should choose first; a useful tip is to measure one of your own garments that is a comfortable fit. Having chosen a size based on width, look at the corresponding length for that size; if you are not happy with the total recommended length, adjust your own garment before beginning your armhole shaping- any adjustment after this point will mean that your sleeve will not fit into your garment easily. Don't forget to take your adjustment into account if there is any side-seam shaping.

GAUGE

Gauge controls both the shape and size of an article, so any variation, however slight, can distort the finished garment.

You must match the gauge given at the start of each pattern. To check your gauge, knit a square in the pattern stitch and/ or stockinette stitch of perhaps 5–10 more stitches and 5–10 more rows than those given in the gauge note. Press the finished square under a damp cloth and mark out the central 4in/10cm square with pins. If you have too many stitches to 4in/10cm, try again using thicker needles. If you have too few stitches to 4in/10cm, try again using finer needles. Once you have achieved the correct gauge, your garment will be knitted to the measurements shown in the size diagram.

CABLE PATTERNS

Cable stitch patterns allow you to twist the stitches in various ways, to create decorative effects such as an interesting rope-like structure to the knitting. The cables can be thin and fine (just a couple of stitches wide) or big and chunky (up to 8 stitches or more).

To work cables, you need to hold the appropriate number of stitches that form the cable twist (abbreviated in pattern as C) on a separate small cable needle, while you knit behind or in front of them. You then knit the stitches off the cable needle before continuing to knit the remaining stitches in the row. Depending on whether the cable needle is at the front or the back of the work, the cables will twist to the left or right but the principle remains the same. A four-stitch cable will be abbreviated as C4F or C4B, depending on whether the cable needle is held to the front or back of the work.

COLORWORK

There are two main methods of working with color in knitted fabrics: the intarsia and the Fairisle techniques.

INTARSIA

In the intarsia technique, you have to join in a new yarn color for each new block of color stitches. To prevent the yarns getting twisted on the ball, the simplest method is to make individual little balls of yarn, or bobbins, from pre-cut short lengths of yarn, one for each motif or block of color used in a row. You then work across the stitches, joining in the colors as required, by twisting them around each other where they meet on the wrong side of the work, to avoid gaps. You will need to neaten up the loose ends. They can either be darned along the color joins or they can be knitted in to the fabric as each color is worked by picking up the loops of the yarns carried across the back of the work as you knit.

FAIRISLE

When you are working a pattern with two or more repeating colors in the same row, you need to strand the yarn not in use behind the stitches being worked. This needs to be done with care, loosely enough to ensure that the strands not in use do not tighten and pucker the front of the knitting. To do this you need to treat the yarns not in use, known as "floating yarns," as if they were one yarn and spread the stitches as you work to their correct width to keep them elastic.

If you tend to knit colorwork too tightly, increase your needle size for the colorwork section.

FINISHING METHODS
PRESSING
Block out each piece of knitting by pinning it on a board to the correct measurements in the pattern. Then lightly press it according to the ball band instructions, omitting any ribbed areas. Take special care to press the edges, as this makes sewing up easier and neater. If you cannot press the fabric, then cover the knitted fabric with a damp cloth and allow it to stand for a couple of hours. Darn in all ends neatly along the selvedge edge or a color join.

STITCHING SEAMS
When you stitch the pieces together, remember to match any areas of color and texture carefully where they meet. Use a special seam stitch, called mattress stitch, as it creates the neatest flattest seam. After all the seams are complete, press the seams and hems. Lastly, sew on the buttons to correspond with the positions of the buttonholes.

ABBREVIATIONS

alt	alternate
approx	approximately
beg	begin(s)(ning)
cm	centimeters
cont	continu(e)(ing)
dec	decreas(e)(ing)
foll(s)	follow(s)(ing)
g	gram
g-st	garter stitch
in	inch(es)
inc	increas(e)(ing)
k	knit
k2tog	knit next 2 sts together
mm	millimeters
M1	make one st by picking up horizontal loop before next st and knitting into back of it
p	purl
patt	pattern
p2tog	purl next 2 sts together
rem	remain(s)(ing)
rep	repeat
RS	right side
skpo	sl 1, k1, pass slipped stitch over
sk2po	sl 1, knit 2 together, pass slipped stitch over
sl 1	slip one st
st(s)	stitch(es)
St st	stockinette stitch (1 row knit, 1 row purl)
tbl	through back of loop(s)
tog	together
WS	wrong side
yd	yard(s)
yo	yarn over
ytf	with yarn to front
ytb	with yarn to back
[ ]/*	repeat instructions within square brackets or between asterisks

Yarn information

The following are the specifications of the Rowan yarns used for the designs in this book. It is always best to try to obtain the exact yarns specified in the patterns, but when substituting yarns, remember to calculate the yarn amount needed by the yardage/meterage rather than by the ball weight. For yarn care directions, refer to the yarn label.

ALPACA COLOUR

Baby alpaca (100 percent); 1¾oz (approximately 131yd/120m) per ball. Recommended gauge: 22 sts and 30 rows to 4in/10cm in St st using size 6 (4mm) knitting needles.

FINE ART

A wool/mohair/silk/polyamide blend yarn; 45 percent wool,/20 percent mohair/10 percent silk/25 percent polyamide; 3½oz (approximately 437yd/400m) per ball. Recommended gauge: 32 sts and 42 rows to 4in/10cm in St st using size 2-3 (2.5-3mm) knitting needles.

FINE ART ARAN

A luxury merino wool/mohair/alpaca/mulberry silk blend yarn; 50 percent wool/20 percent mohair/5 percent silk/25 percent alpaca; 3½oz (approximately 186yd/170m) per ball. Recommended gauge: 19 sts and 25 rows to 4in/10cm in St st using size 7 (4.5mm) knitting needles.

KID CLASSIC

A lambswool-mohair-polyamide mix yarn (70 percent lambswool, 25 percent kid mohair, 4 percent polyamide); 1¾oz (153yd/140m) per ball. Recommended gauge: 18-19 sts and 23-25 rows to 4in/10cm in St st using size 8-9 (5-5.5mm) knitting needles.

KIDSILK HAZE

A fine-weight mohair mix yarn; 70 percent super kid mohair, 30 percent silk; 1oz (approximately 229yd/210m) per ball. Recommended gauge: 18-25 sts and 23-34 rows to 4in/10cm in St st using sizes 3-8 (3.25-5mm) knitting needles.

PURE WOOL 4PLY

Wool (100 percent); 1¾oz (approximately 174yd/160m) per ball. Recommended gauge: 28 sts and 36 rows to 4in/10cm in St st using size 3 (3.25mm) knitting needles.

WOOL COTTON

A wool/cotton blend yarn; 50 percent merino wool, 50 percent cotton; 1¾oz (approximately 123yd/113m) per ball. Recommended gauge: 22-24 sts and 30-32 rows to 4in/10cm in St st using size 5-6 (3.75-4mm) knitting needles.

WOOL COTTON 4PLY

A wool/cotton blend yarn; 50 percent merino wool, 50 percent cotton; 1¾oz (197yd/180m) per ball. Recommended gauge: 28 sts and 36 rows to 4in/10cm in St st using size 2 (3.25mm) knitting needles.

Suppliers

U.S.A.
Westminster Fibers,
8 Shelter Drive, Greer
South Carolina 29650
www.westminsterfibers.com

U.K.
Rowan, Green Lane Mill, Holmfirth,
West Yorkshire HD9 2DX
www.knitrowan.com

AUSTRALIA
Australian Country Spinners Pty Ltd,
Melbourne, Victoria 3004
customerservice@auspinners.com.au

AUSTRIA
Coats Harlander GesmbH
1210 Vienna
www.coatscrafts.at

BELGIUM
Coats GmbH, 79341 Kenzingen
www.coatscrafts.be

BULGARIA
Coats Bulgaria
BG-1784 Sofia
www.coatsbulgaria.bg

CANADA
Westminster Fibers
Vaughan, Ontario L4H 3M8
info@westminsterfibers.com

CHINA
Coats Shanghai Ltd, Shanghai
victor.li@coats.com

CYPRUS
Coats Bulgaria
BG-1784 Sofia
www.coatscrafts.com.cy

CZECH REPUBLIC
Coats Czecho
s.r.o.Staré Mesto 246 569 32
galanterie@coats.com

DENMARK
Carl J. Permin A/S Egegaardsvej
28 DK-2610 Rødovre
permin@permin.dk

ESTONIA
Coats Eesti AS, Ampri tee 9/4,
74001 Viimsi Harjumaa
www.coatscrafts.co.ee

FINLAND
Coats Opti Crafts Oy, Kerava 04200
www.coatscrafts.fi

FRANCE
Coats GmbH, 79341 Kenzingen
www.coatscrafts.fr

GERMANY
Coats GmbH, 79341 Kenzingen
www.coatsgmbh.de

GREECE
Coats Bulgaria
BG-1784 Sofia
www.coatscrafts.gr

HOLLAND
See Belgium

HONG KONG
East Unity Company Ltd, Chai Wan
eastunityco@yahoo.com.hk

ICELAND
Storkurinn, Reykjavik 101
storkurinn@simnet.is

ITALY
Coats Cucirini srl, Milan 20126
www.coatscucirini.com

KOREA
Coats Korea Co. Ltd, Seoul 137-060
rozenpark@coats.com

LATVIA
Coats Latvija SIA, Mukusalas str.
41 b, Riga LV-1004
www.coatscrafts.lv

LEBANON
y.knot, Saifi Village, Beirut
y.knot@cyberia.net.lb

LITHUANIA & RUSSIA
Coats Lietuva UAB,
LT-09310 Vilnius
www.coatscrafts.lt

LUXEMBOURG
See Belgium

MALTA
John Gregory Ltd, 8 Ta'Xbiex Sea
Front, Msida MSD 1512
raygreg@onvol.ne

MEXICO
Estambres Crochet SA de CV, Aaron
Saenz 1891-7,64650 MONTERREY
+52 (81) 8335-3870

NEW ZEALAND
ACS New Zealand, Christchurch
lynn@impactmg.co.nz

NORWAY
See Denmark

PORTUGAL
Coats & Clark, Quinta de Cravel,
Apartado 444, 4431-968
00 351 223 770700

SINGAPORE
Golden Dragon Store,
Singapore 058357
gdscraft@hotmail.com

SLOVAKIA
Coats s.r.o.Kopcianska 94851 01
Bratislava
galanteria@coats.com

SOUTH AFRICA
Arthur Bales Ltd,
Johannesburg 2195
arthurb@new.co.za

SPAIN
Coats Fabra SAU,
08027 Barcelona
atencion.clientes@coats.com

SWEDEN
See Denmark

SWITZERLAND
Coats Stroppel AG,
Untersiggenthal 5417
www.coatscrafts.ch

TAIWAN
Cactus Quality Co Ltd,
Taiwan, R.O.C. 10084
cqcl@ms17.hinet.net

THAILAND
Global Wide Trading,
Bangkok 10310
global.wide@yahoo.com

For stockists in all other
countries please contact Rowan
for details

Acknowledgments

AUTHOR'S ACKNOWLEDGMENTS

A huge and heartfelt thank you to the following team of people: Steven and Susan for their fabulous work on the photography, art direction and styling; Emma G, Harriet, and Sogol for modeling so beautifully; Anne, for her sublime page layouts; our fabulous pattern writer, Penny Hill, and her team of wonderful knitters; Frances for the beautifully knitted swatches; Katie and Marilyn for their diligent editing and pattern checking; and the entire Rowan team for their continuous support.

PUBLISHERS' ACKNOWLEDGMENTS

Many thanks to everyone who worked on this book. In addition to the team mentioned by Martin, we would also like to Therese Chynoweth for the charts, Light Locations for the location, 12+ model agency and, of course, the models themselves.